D1133663

ONE HUNDRED YEARS OF IDAHO ART 1850-1950

Summer 2003
Barbara and Leon.
With love for Foote and Family,
thanks for the talk and memories.
Love, Kay.

LENDERS TO THE EXHIBITION

Mrs. R. W. Addison

Marcia Anderson

Amon Carter Museum
Fort Worth, Texas

Don Aupperle

Don Bemco Bennett

Mr. and Mrs. Frank Blanchard

John P. Blanchard

Doran Butler

Idaho City Historical Foundation, Inc.

Boise Public Library

Boise State University
Hemingway Western Studies Center

Buffalo Bill Historical Center
Cody, Wyoming

Burbank Family

Burlington Resources
Seattle, Washington

Mr. and Mrs. Joseph A. Chester

Cheney Cowles Museum
Spokane, Washington

College of Idaho
Rosenthal Gallery
Caldwell, Idaho

Cooper-Hewitt Museum,
The Smithsonian Institution's
National Museum of Design
New York

Alfred C. Dunn

Cornelia Hart Farrer

Mr. and Mrs. Philip Fast

The Thomas Gilcrease Institute
of American History and Art
Tulsa, Oklahoma

Judge Alfred C. Hagan

John C. Hoover

Hummel, LaMarche & Hunsucker, Architects, P.A.
Boise, Idaho

Idaho State Historical Society
Boise, Idaho

Idaho State University
Student Union Permanent Art Collection
Pocatello, Idaho

Kennedy Galleries, Inc.
New York

Mr. and Mrs. John Kirby

Mary Kirkwood

Latah County Historical Society
Moscow, Idaho

Library of Congress
Washington, D.C.

National Archives
Washington, D.C.

National Gallery of Art
Washington, D.C.

National Museum of American Art
Smithsonian Institution
Washington, D.C.

National Park Service
Grand Teton National Park
Moose, Wyoming

Nez Perce National Historical Park
Spalding, Idaho

Peabody Museum of Archaeology and Ethnology
Harvard University
Cambridge, Massachusetts

Betty Penson-Ward

George Roberts

Roswell Museum & Art Center
Roswell, New Mexico

Larry Schoonover

Sidestreet Gallery
Sandpoint, Idaho

William and Genevra Sloan

Jack Spurgeon

Carolyn Staley Fine Prints
Seattle, Washington

State Historical Society of Wisconsin
Madison, Wisconsin

University of Idaho
Lionel Hampton School of Music
Moscow, Idaho

University of Idaho Library
Moscow, Idaho

University of Maryland College Park
College Park, Maryland

University of Puget Sound
Tacoma, Washington

Washington State University Libraries
Pullman, Washington

Dale Walden

Arnold Westerlund

Larry Meierotto and Mary Abercrombie

Robert S. Meyer

Museum of Church History & Art
Salt Lake City, Utah

Museum of Fine Arts
Boston, Massachusetts

Museum of Native American Cultures
Spokane, Washington

National Anthropological Archives
Smithsonian Institution
Washington, D.C.

ONE HUNDRED YEARS OF IDAHO ART 1850-1950

BOISE ART MUSEUM

JUNE 23 - AUGUST 19, 1990

SANDY HARTHORN
AND
KATHLEEN BETTIS

A CENTENNIAL EXHIBITION AND CATALOG
SUPPORTED WITH GRANTS FROM:

ALBERTSON'S, INC.
BEAUX ARTS SOCIÉTÉ
IDAHO CENTENNIAL COMMISSION
IDAHO HUMANITIES COUNCIL
KEY BANK OF IDAHO
NATIONAL ENDOWMENT FOR THE ARTS

CREDITS

ESSAYS AND CURATION: SANDY HARTHORN
RESEARCH AND BIOGRAPHIES: KATHLEEN BETTIS
DESIGN: GEOFFREY BEARD
TYPOGRAPHER: IMAGE PROJECTIONS, INC
PRINTER: JOSLYN AND MORRIS, INC., BOISE, IDAHO
PRINTED IN THE USA

LIBRARY OF CONGRESS:

HARTHORN, SANDY, 1945-
ONE HUNDRED YEARS OF IDAHO ART, 1850-1950: JUNE 23 - AUGUST 19, 1990 / BY SANDY HARTHORN AND KATHLEEN BETTIS.

P. CM.

"AN IDAHO CENTENNIAL EXHIBITION ORGANIZED BY THE BOISE ART MUSEUM"—VERSO T.P.

INCLUDES BIBLIOGRAPHICAL REFERENCES AND INDEX.

1. ART, AMERICAN—IDAHO—EXHIBITIONS. 2. ART, MODERN—19TH CENTURY—IDAHO—EXHIBITIONS. 3. ART. MODERN—20TH CENTURY—IDAHO—EXHIBITIONS. 4. IDAHO IN ART— EXHIBITIONS. I. BETTIS, KATHLEEN, 1947- . II. BOISE ART MUSEUM. III. TITLE.

N6530.I2H37 1990
709'.796'07479628—DC20

90-808
CIP

THIS EXHIBITION AND CATALOG ARE SUPPORTED BY A SPECIAL EXHIBITIONS GRANT FROM THE NATIONAL ENDOWMENT FOR THE ARTS, WASHINGTON, D.C.

MUSEUM PROGRAMS ARE PRESENTED WITH SUPPORT OF THE IDAHO COMMISSION ON THE ARTS AND THE NATIONAL ENDOWMENT FOR THE ARTS, WASHINGTON, D.C.; AND THROUGH A GRANT FROM THE INSTITUTE OF MUSEUM SERVICES, A FEDERAL AGENCY THAT OFFERS GENERAL OPERATING SUPPORT TO THE NATION'S MUSEUMS.

THIS PROGRAM IS SUPPORTED IN PART BY A GRANT FROM THE IDAHO HUMANITIES COUNCIL, A STATE-BASED PROGRAM OF THE NATIONAL ENDOWMENT FOR THE HUMANITIES. THE CONCLUSIONS OR OPINIONS IN THIS CATALOG DO NOT NECESSARILY REPRESENT THE VIEWS OF EITHER THE IDAHO HUMANITIES COUNCIL OR THE NATIONAL ENDOWMENT FOR THE HUMANITIES.

FRONT COVER:

ROBERT W. ADDISON
VIEW OF BOISE
1949
OIL ON CANVAS
25½" × 29¾"
COLLECTION MRS. ROBERT W. ADDISON

CONTENTS

INTRODUCTION
4

FIRST ENCOUNTERS
7

INITIAL VISIONS
24

BUILDING A STATE
60

A STEP TOWARD PROGRESS
78

EXHIBITION CHECKLIST
117

SELECTED BIBLIOGRAPHY
128

INDEX
131

ACKNOWLEDGMENTS
132

INTRODUCTION

In 1986, with the commencement of the State Centennial celebration, the Boise Art Museum was given the opportunity to prepare the first comprehensive historical exhibition of Idaho artwork. As research on Idaho artists was initially compiled, preconceptions that information and surviving artwork would be limited were soon challenged. The documentation on both amateur and professional artists who had worked in the state proved to be substantial. Moreover, it soon became evident that each period of artistic production was integrally related to the history of settlement and economic growth in the state. Art in Idaho is, in fact, a mirror of territorial and state development. The images ultimately chosen for *One Hundred Years of Idaho Art: 1850 - 1950* not only illustrate the stages of the state's maturation, but represent the best available works by those artists who lived in and traveled throughout the boundaries of what is present-day Idaho.

The objective of this exhibition is to provide an overview of the art in the state beginning with its initial explorers and visitors. The period from 1850 to 1950 was adopted, rather than Idaho's state centennial years, in order to include important renderings produced by early western travelers. As research progressed, it became apparent that the exhibit would be considerably more meaningful if the time frame was extended to span 120 years, from the 1837 views of Alfred Jacob Miller to compositions completed during the mid-1950s. In some instances, later depictions were selected in order to offer examples by artists whose earlier pieces are no longer available.

Exhibition research identified more than three hundred artists who had at one time been active in Idaho and were mentioned in newspaper articles, books, or other references. Additional inquiries were made to historical societies, museums, galleries, and private collectors. Because more material was uncovered than anticipated, and because it was not possible to include representations by all of the artists, we chose to focus upon individuals whose works in some way epitomized art in the region during the years of territorial and state expansion. Conscious effort has been made to highlight artists whose work relates directly to Idaho's social and cultural evolution, rather than those who merely by circumstance of their birth lived in the state.

As particular works by this broad-ranging group of artists were selected for the exhibition, several additional factors were weighed. Pieces were considered for inclusion if the image was of an Idaho location or subject, particularly if it was created within the state. Others were chosen because they exemplify the work of artists whose careers evolved in Idaho. While the largest cache of Idaho artwork is owned by the Idaho State Historical Society, many objects were discovered at other public institutions and through private collectors. On occasion, an artist's work was untraceable. Unfortunately, over the years, some artworks have been cast aside or given away because they were not considered to be of importance by owners, artists' families, or dealers.

The exhibition, now compiled as *One Hundred Years of Idaho Art: 1850 - 1950*, is a collection of over two hundred paintings, drawings, prints, and photographs of the state: images recorded through the eyes of Idahoans, as well as other American artists, who came here to describe Idaho's magnificent landscapes, growing communities, and historical figures. The exhibition catalog offers biographical information and pertinent anecdotes regarding these artists and their subjects. In ninety essays on individual artists, we have attempted to explore not only their personal backgrounds, but the stories behind their images. In both the exhibition and catalog, we have sought to interpret the character of Idaho art in the context of various periods: exploration, pioneer days, the mining and gold rush era, years of political and cultural growth, the Depression era, and post-war years.

In celebrating the first century of Idaho art, this exhibition traces art in the state from the earliest representations by explorers to the emergence of modern artistic styles. The first hundred years, from approximately 1850 to 1950, laid the foundation for future accomplishments. The next hundred years, 1950 to 2050, will establish Idaho's artistic traditions. As art is always a reflection of the times in which it is created, the first hundred years tell the story of tenacious survival and record optimistic beginnings.

Sandy Harthorn
Kathleen Bettis

ALFRED JACOB MILLER
PIERRE—A ROCKY MOUNTAIN TRAPPER
CIRCA 1837
PENCIL, PEN, INK, WASH & GOUACHE ON PAPER
$6^{3}/_{4} \times 9^{1}/_{4}$"
COLLECTION THE THOMAS GILCREASE INSTITUTE OF AMERICAN HISTORY AND ART, TULSA, OKLAHOMA

FIRST ENCOUNTERS

No boundaries existed for the state of Idaho when explorers, mountain men, missionaries, and immigrants first considered making the long trek west. Located beyond the far reaches of the Rocky Mountains, Idaho was yet to be systematically explored at the beginning of the nineteenth century. Its terrain was difficult to penetrate, inhabited by Indians, and reported to have unusual geologic characteristics quite unlike geographic features found in the East. Early written accounts emphasized the exotic nature of the country, with its vast and spectacular landscapes and fascinating native population.

The first official overland expeditions to journey through the interior of the Pacific Northwest departed up the Missouri River to survey the enormous land area acquired from France under the provisions of the Louisiana Purchase. Lewis and Clark arrived at the Pacific Coast in 1805, crossing the Bitteroots through Lolo Pass into what is presently Idaho, where they first encountered Nez Perce Indians below the south fork of the Clearwater River. They returned with a wealth of information and scientific data and their reports of the western territories fired the imagination of easterners and sparked a desire for additional description and exploration.

Within ten years of Lewis and Clark's venture, the first American fur post west of the Rocky Mountains was founded at Fort Henry on the headwaters of the Snake River, and soon thereafter, the Pacific Fur Company sent trapping expeditions up the Snake and along its tributaries in search of beaver and other pelts. By the time Catholic and Protestant missionaries entered the area in the 1830s, the Rocky Mountain Fur Company and the Hudson Bay Company had established trading posts in the region of present-day southern Idaho.

Nicholas Point, a missionary and first practicing artist to depict Idaho, accompanied the Jesuit priest Pierre Jean De Smet to the Northwest in 1841. They passed through Fort Hall, the Hudson Bay Company's settlement, which served as an inland trading post and way station. Point's journal drawings, executed on this trip, give us a firsthand look at the sprawling plains that would become the entryway to southeastern Idaho. By 1842, merely a decade after the era when Indians and a small number of mountain men were Idaho's sole inhabitants, the route followed by early trappers and missionaries had become a well-traveled passage to the West — the Oregon Trail.

During the mid-nineteenth century, the United States Government sponsored the majority of expeditions to explore unknown regions of the Northwest. Their initial goal was to discover and chart rivers and drainage systems that might provide access to the Pacific Ocean. Surveyors were assigned to measure, describe and map the area in order that the government and public could begin to evaluate, understand, and eventually develop the resources of the Pacific Northwest.

Beginning in the 1840s, expeditions to the Far West were usually accompanied by artists. Charles Preuss, traveling with John C. Fremont's 1843-44 survey party, was probably the first artist to record Idaho's scenic wonders in an official capacity. In 1849, George Gibbs and William Henry Tappan, both civilian artists, followed the Oregon Trail with the Regiment of United States Mounted Riflemen. The spectacular scenery witnessed by these artist-explorers was recorded in illustrated government reports, and their graphic descriptions of the West were among the first to be published. With growing public curiosity and enthusiasm for the West, as well as strengthening Congressional support for further exploration, the number of artist-travelers on the westward highway increased significantly during the 1850s.

Professional artists who first accompanied explorers and surveyors were retained to portray the geological, topographical, and biological subjects encountered, as well as the indigenous inhabitants. The majority of these artists were trained in Europe and their artwork reflects the influences of popular continental styles. The beginning of westward expansion coincided with European Romantic movements in art and literature. Romantic ideals were associated with a belief in the supremacy of nature and the innate goodness of primitive man, concepts espoused by French philosopher Jean Jacques Rousseau. The dramatic idea of man measured against the awesome untamed expanse of the West, and the Romantic notion of the purity of Indian life existing in close proximity to nature were both concepts which appealed to professional artists of the period.

ASHER B. DURAND
KINDRED SPIRITS
1849
OIL ON CANVAS
44 x 36"
COURTESY NEW YORK PUBLIC LIBRARY
ASTOR, LENOX AND TILDEN FOUNDATIONS

For the most part, the artists who came into what is now Idaho in the mid-nineteenth century had some previous academic training. Because of their generally similar educational backgrounds, the "genre of the art produced by explorers during the 1840s and 1850s was a combination of romantic view painting and topographical renditions with pretensions to scientific accuracy."[1] Artists who accompanied the surveys and exploratory expeditions generally worked in pencil, ink, or watercolor, mediums that were especially appropriate for rough working conditions. For artists journeying by wagon or on horseback, watercolor was particularly well suited, because in addition to its ease of transport and use, it made possible the rapid execution of color sketches while the details and intensity of a scene were fresh in the artist's mind. Moreover, the translucent quality of the medium adapted well to the description of the transitory effects of light and atmosphere found in the bright western sky.

By the early 1850s, three primary themes came to "dominate the iconography of the Pacific Northwest: exotic Indian culture, stories of pioneer progress, and stunning larger-than-life scenery."[2] In Idaho, George Catlin and Gustavus Sohon were among the first artists to portray native Americans in their homeland, while James Wilkins was one of the earliest to visually record the actual wagon migration west. Although most artists of this period worked on relatively small paper, necessitated by the inconvenience of travel, they presented their subjects in a grand-scale fashion. Landscapes, such as those seen in the work of James Alden and Charles Preuss, emphasize great distance and spacious skies.

In the east there was a national awakening with regard to the American heritage. The Hudson River School of landscape painting popularized images of the American wilderness, exalting its grandeur and aura of mystery. Eastern artists sought to find new sources of idealized splendor in the West and were not disappointed. "Artists went out into the West with the idea of accurate documentation in mind, but so stunned were they by what they saw—they inevitably produced romanticized interpretations."[3] This effect, sometimes seen in early Idaho works, is noted in John Mix Stanley's sentimental interpretation of the Snake River. In another small canvas, by Emma Coleman, the artist naively captures the nostalgia of Asher B. Durand's famous oil

C. EMMA COLEMAN
VALLEY OF SALUBRIA
CIRCA 1870
OIL ON CANVAS
16⅛ × 13⅛" OVAL
COLLECTION IDAHO STATE HISTORICAL SOCIETY

painting *Kindred Spirits*, which perpetuated the myth of a natural, unspoiled paradise and magnified the perception of the West as an idealized and romantic place.

Before 1860, Idaho was a wild, virtually unsettled region of varied terrain bisected by formidable mountains and the natural barriers of deep canyons and cascading rivers. After traders and missionaries built the first settlements, and westward routes were established through Indian lands, the way was opened to an influx of easterners looking for opportunities and a new life in the West. For the majority of adventurers, Idaho was not the destination, but a territory to be traversed on the way to the Pacific Coast. It was not until forts were constructed, military personnel were installed to protect travelers, and ferry crossings and way stations were in place, that a few settlers began to stay. Until that time, artistic images of Idaho consisted of impressions recorded by pathfinders documenting the overland experience.

1. Goetzmann, William H., and William N. Goetzmann. *The West of the Imagination* (New York: Norton, 1986) 102
2. Goetzmann, William H. *Looking at the Land of Promise* (Pullman, Washington: Washington State University Press, 1988) 29
3. Goetzmann. *The West of the Imagination*, 103

ALFRED JACOB MILLER

ALFRED JACOB MILLER
SNAKE INDIAN
CIRCA 1837
PENCIL AND WATERCOLOR ON PAPER
5½ × 4½"
COLLECTION BUFFALO BILL HISTORICAL CENTER
CODY, WYOMING
BEQUEST OF JOSEPH M. ROEBLING

In 1837, Alfred Jacob Miller was hired by Captain William Drummond Stewart, a Scottish nobleman and adventurer, to illustrate "the remarkable scenery and incidents" on an American Fur Company expedition into the far reaches of the West. They traveled nearly to the eastern boundary of what is now Idaho, to the trappers' rendezvous at Green River.

Two other artists, Karl Bodmer and George Catlin, preceded Miller to the wilderness, but neither traveled so far into the interior nor painted episodes of the fur trade and life in the Rocky Mountains. Miller's abundant body of work gave easterners their first view of the Shoshone, Snake, Bannock, and Nez Perce tribes who then inhabited the unexplored areas of this western frontier.

Miller trained as a portrait painter, studied under the American artist Thomas Sully and attended the Ecole des Beaux-Arts in Paris during the 1830s. Taking an opportunity to study the old masters, he sketched at the Louvre and was inspired by European painting styles and Romantic concepts espousing the return to nature and the innate goodness of man. The characteristics of Romantic thought, including the exaltation of the "noble savage," adapted well to the subject matter of the American West.

Native Americans were the primary subjects of Miller's oeuvre. His fascination for tribal cultures encompassed the description of their homelands, customs, and individual appearance. Miller, who chose his subjects because of their beauty or character, especially admired Indians whose features and stature reminded him of classical sculpture. In keeping with Romantic principles, Miller often depicted Native Americans in the nostalgic setting of an arcadian wilderness. Not concerned with a literal view of the West, Miller nonetheless succeeds in conveying a sense of untouched hinterlands and the spirit of Rocky Mountain life before the encroachment of settlers.

Born January 2, 1810, in Baltimore. Educated in Baltimore; may have studied art with the Peale family. Studied portraiture under Thomas Sully, 1831-32. Studied at the Ecole des Beaux-Arts, Paris, and at the English Life School in Rome, 1833-34. Returned to open a portrait studio in Baltimore, then in New Orleans. Traveled with the expedition of Captain William Drummond Stewart of the British Army to the Rocky Mountain fur trappers' rendezvous of 1837, returning to New Orleans in the autumn. Prepared oil paintings of the expedition for Captain Stewart's castle in Scotland and exhibited them in Baltimore in 1838, in New York in 1839. Traveled in Scotland and England, 1840-42. Returned to Baltimore and continued his painting career there until his death, June 26, 1874.

NICOLAS POINT

Jesuit missionaries were responsible for establishing the first church settlements among the Flathead and Coeur d'Alene Indians of northern Idaho and Montana. In 1841 six missionaries and a caravan of travelers arrived in the Northwest under the leadership of Father Pierre Jean De Smet, a Catholic priest and diplomat. Accompanying De Smet was Father Nicolas Point, a French artist and architect, who helped organize the missions and acted as official diarist for the party. The Jesuits' evangelistic efforts exposed the northern tribes to European values, customs and Christian beliefs which profoundly changed their native way of life and worship.

The De Smet expedition came across the Bear River Mountains to Fort Hall, where they were met by a contingent of Flathead Indians who escorted them into the Bitterroot Basin. After founding a mission in Montana, the Jesuits established a site among the Coeur d'Alene Indians near St. Maries on the St. Joe River. Because the land was subject to frequent flooding, the church site was moved to a more suitable location above the Coeur d'Alene River. Here Father Point lived and worked among the Indians from 1840 to 1846. Known as the Coeur d'Alene Mission of the Sacred Heart and later as the Cataldo Mission, this structure is Idaho's oldest standing building.

Nicolas Point's journal illustrates the expedition's passage west, the construction of the missions, and facets of Indian culture. Point worked in a quaint simple manner,

Born April 10, 1799, in Rocroy, France. Joined the Society of Jesus in 1819 in order to become a missionary. Ordained to the priesthood in 1831; served in Jesuit colleges in Switzerland and Spain. Came to America in 1834. Taught at St. Mary's, Kentucky; established St. Charles College at Grand Coteau, Louisiana, 1838-40. Joined Father Pierre Jean De Smet in establishing St. Mary's Mission among the Flatheads, at the present Stevensville, Montana. Opened Sacred Heart Mission among the Coeur d'Alene Indians, 1842. Continued to evangelize the Flatheads on buffalo-hunting trips, worked among the Blackfeet at Ft. Lewis. Returned east in 1847; headed a mission in Ontario, Canada, until 1859. Retired near Montreal to compose his Recollections of the Rocky Mountains, *illustrated with portraits and scenes of Northwest Indian life. Died in Quebec July 4, 1868, and is buried in the Quebec cathedral crypt.*

NICOLAS POINT
INTERIEUR DE L'EGLISE DU SACRE COEUR
CHEZ LES COEUR D'ALENES
1842
WATERCOLOR, PENCIL, AND INK ON PAPER
4½ × 6½"
PIERRE JEAN DE SMET PAPERS
COLLECTION WASHINGTON STATE UNIVERSITY LIBRARIES

noting the indigenous names of land formations and descriptions of the native inhabitants. His graphite drawings convey a talent and propensity for drawing, but his awkward handling of perspective and anatomy betray a lack of technical knowledge. In one of his few interior drawings, he portrays the inside of the Chapel of the Sacred Heart during the Christmas observances of 1842. He shows the interior of the church decorated for midnight mass, adorned with green garlands and the choir hung with ritual tapestries.

Nicolas Point is remembered as a patient, kind, and gentle man whose sketches of the Pacific Northwest were ultimately used to illustrate books written by the pioneer Jesuit missionary Pierre De Smet. These pictorial documents give us an extensive record of Jesuit activity among the Indians in the remote north before the advent of eastern immigrations to the Oregon Territory.

NICOLAS POINT
VIEW OF THE MISSION ESTABLISHMENT IN 1846 AMONG THE POINTED-HEARTS
1846
ENGRAVING
4½ × 7½"
PIERRE JEAN DE SMET PAPERS
COLLECTION WASHINGTON STATE UNIVERSITY LIBRARIES

JAMES F. WILKINS

JAMES F. WILKINS
DESCENT OF BEAR RIVER MOUNTAINS
AUGUST 1, 1849
MONOCHROME WASH DRAWING ON PAPER
8½ × 10"
ICONOGRAPHIC COLLECTIONS
STATE HISTORICAL SOCIETY OF WISCONSIN

Born in England, 1808. Exhibited miniatures in 1835-36 at the Royal Academy, London. Came to America around 1837 and painted in Peoria, Illinois, New Orleans, and St. Louis. Joined wagon train to California, leaving Weston, Missouri, in May 1849. Returned from San Francisco in December via steamship. Worked for several months in Peoria on a large-scale panorama, which was shown in Peoria, St. Louis, Cincinnati, Louisville, and Frankfort, Kentucky. Lived in the St. Louis area 1850-1872, painting portraits, genre scenes, western landscapes and literary subjects. Purchased a farm near Shobonier, Fayette Co., Illinois, and lived there until his death June 18, 1888.

James Wilkins' scheme to create an immense "moving panorama of the Oregon Trail" was a wildly ambitious enterprise. It was a stupendous idea for a miniature portrait painter to create a thousand-foot-long painting which would describe the landscape along the entire length of the main passage west from the Missouri River to California. With this plan in mind, however, Wilkins departed from St. Louis with an ox-drawn wagon caravan in the spring of 1849.

Wilkins set down in his journal not only the scenery and incidents of the five-month journey, but also the grueling difficulties of travel along the rutted and mud-tracked stretches of this famous trail. Of particular interest to Idahoans are Wilkins' drawings of the hazardous descent over the Bear River Mountains into the southeast corner of what is now Idaho. On Wednesday, August 1, 1849, Wilkins notes in his diary: "We started at sunrise being obliged to...ascend and descend the mountain, the steepest and longest ascent we have made on the route....I made a sketch of the descent, but owing to the clouds of dust, it was anything but pleasant to sit sketching."[1] In his drawing, the wagons are shown winding their way down the rough mountain crossing to the valley below, where relative ease of travel could once again be enjoyed.

Upon arrival in California, Wilkins hastily booked a ship back to the East Coast to organize production of his panorama. Months of time and technical assistance were required: "a picture nine or ten feet high and four or five hundred yards long was not to be finished overnight."[2] Wilkins completed the panorama project and within a year the three-reel canvas painting, prepared from notebook images of the trip, had received an enthusiastic reception in St. Louis and several other cities. Although the present whereabouts of the panorama is unknown and it may no longer exist, Wilkins' original journal drawings reflect a fresh personal experience of life on the trail and give us a striking pictorial record of the rugged descent over the Bear River Mountains into the Soda Springs area of southern Idaho.

1. Wilkins, James F. *An Artist on the Oregon Trail: The 1849 Diary and Sketches of James F. Wilkins* (San Marino: The Huntington Library, 1968) 60.
2. Wilkins 12.

CHARLES PREUSS

CHARLES PREUSS
AMERICAN FALLS OF LEWIS FORK
1845
LITHOGRAPH
5 × 7½"
COLLECTION IDAHO STATE HISTORICAL SOCIETY
LIBRARY AND ARCHIVES

One of the first to visually record the landscape beyond the Rocky Mountains was Charles Preuss, a cartographer trained in Europe who worked as a surveyor for the Prussian government before immigrating to the United States in 1834. Because of his invaluable map-making credentials, he was initially employed by the U.S. Coast Survey, and was later recommended as a cartographer to John C. Fremont. From 1842 to 1844, detachments of the Army Corps of Topographical Engineers under Fremont's command explored and charted what was to become the immigration road to the Oregon Territory. Preuss prepared the first maps of the vast domain beyond the Missouri River based on modern principles of geodesy and cartography.

Although Preuss was not trained as an artist, he executed a number of sketches while on the trail, including a view of American Falls, one of the first glimpses of what is now eastern Idaho. *American Falls of Lewis Fork* was drawn September 24, 1843. We have not only the visual image, but his accompanying diary exclamation jotted on the scene: "A wild country! How old man Vulcan has played havoc here—a little mythology is quite proper. I sketched a rather pretty waterfall today."[1] Phrased in heroic terms, it is a description clearly inspired by the unearthly nature of the spring-filled volcanic region.

Because Preuss was trained as a cartographer and not an artist, we can accept that his rather naive drawings outline the land features rather than describe them as solid forms. Drawn in a stiff awkward manner, this deep vista appears exaggerated and fanciful. The river drops from a flattened plain over the edge of an angulated precipice more illusory than real.

The original drawings are long lost, but still intact are the lithographic prints illustrating Fremont's reports of the first and second expeditions. Standing in the shadow of Fremont, Preuss is recognized for his years of valuable service and his role as the first scientific mapmaker of America's western interior.

Born April 30, 1803, in Hoehscheid, Germany. Trained in geodesy and cartography. Arrived in America in 1834. Employed by the U.S. Coast Survey. Served as cartographer on the first, second, and fourth of John C. Fremont's exploring expeditions through the Rocky Mountains, Oregon Territory, Pacific Coast, and Southwest, 1842-1849. Commissioned by the U.S. Senate in 1847 to construct a map of Oregon, Upper California, and the central Rockies. Worked as a surveyor in California, 1849-50, before returning to Washington, D.C. Surveyed again in California in 1853 with the Pacific Railroad Survey. Became despondent over illness which curtailed his western field work; committed suicide near Washington, September 1, 1854.

1. Preuss, Charles. *Exploring with Fremont* (Norman: University of Oklahoma Press, 1958) 91.

GEORGE GIBBS, JR.

Two talented civilian draftsmen, William Henry Tappan and George Gibbs, accompanied the U.S. Army's Regiment of Mounted Riflemen west on the Oregon Trail in 1849. The party was appointed to organize posts for the establishment of order along the route and to take possession of the army post at Fort Vancouver. This notable military campaign became known as the Cross Expedition, named after quartermaster Major Osborne Cross, who logged the records of the trip.

At the age of twenty-seven, William Henry Tappan had already explored Lake Superior and the Platte River sections of the Midwest. He was a professional engraver who adapted photographs to mezzotints, engraved line plates, and had been employed as a draftsman for the U.S. Mint. Keenly interested in the exploration of the frontier, he obtained permission to travel with the Mounted Riflemen over the Oregon Trail. His assignment included gathering zoological and botanical specimens and drawing geological features. Covering the breadth of present-day Idaho, the troop came across South Pass to the Bear River and then on to Fort Hall and Fort Boise. Tappan's sketches of the two forts are the earliest interior and exterior views of these historic Idaho landmarks.

George Gibbs was a Harvard graduate in law and a talented artist intensely attracted to the natural history and indigenous cultures of the West. During the trek

Born near Astoria, Long Island, on July 17, 1815. Studied in Europe, graduated from Harvard University in 1838. Worked as an attorney; also a writer and natural historian. Joined Company of Mounted Riflemen at Fort Leavenworth and traveled the Oregon Trail, 1849. Developed expertise in Pacific Northwestern Indian languages and cultures, writing vocabularies, collecting artifacts for the Smithsonian, and assisting in treaty negotiations. Prepared maps for Isaac Stevens' Pacific Railroad Survey; served as astronomer and ethnologist in 1857 on the Northwest Boundary Commission. Returned to the East Coast in 1860, living near Washington, D.C. Moved to New Haven, Connecticut, in 1871. Died at New Haven April 19, 1873.

GEORGE GIBBS
SHOSHONE FALLS OF SNAKE RIVER,
AUG. 15, 1849, FROM BELOW
PENCIL ON PAPER
5³/₈ × 8³/₈"
COLLECTION PEABODY MUSEUM OF ARCHAEOLOGY
AND ETHNOLOGY, HARVARD UNIVERSITY

WILLIAM HENRY TAPPAN

Born October 30, 1821, at Manchester, Massachusetts. Worked as an engraver in Boston and Philadelphia in the 1840s. Member of Lake Superior exploration party of Louis Agassiz, 1848. Traveled in Platte River area. Joined Company of Mounted Riflemen at Fort Kearny and traveled the Oregon Trail, 1849. Lived at St. Helen's, Oregon Territory, 1851-54. Credited with designing and engraving the Seal of Washington Territory. Became Columbia River District Indian agent in 1855; took part in treaty negotiations at Walla Walla. Moved to Colorado and worked as a storekeeper, 1850-1876. Returned to Massachusetts and served in the legislature. Died January 22, 1907.

across southern Idaho, Gibbs took a side trip with several army officers to visit Shoshone Falls. From a vantage point at the base of the falls, Gibbs made a quick rendering to record this natural phenomenon. In this straightforward sketch, the rainbow arching across the falls compositionally links the vertical basalt walls of this deep-worn canyon.

Major Cross's 1850 report of the Mounted Riflemen's journey became a vital factual source for subsequent travelers, so much in demand that it required three editions. The published report was illustrated with lithographs that constituted the first official and extensive pictorial record of the Oregon Trail, showing its passage through southern Idaho to the Pacific.

WILLIAM TAPPAN
INSIDE VIEW OF FORT HALL
1850
LITHOGRAPH
5 × 8″
COLLECTION IDAHO STATE HISTORICAL SOCIETY
LIBRARY AND ARCHIVES

GEORGE CATLIN

GEORGE CATLIN
A CROW VILLAGE AND THE SALMON RIVER MOUNTAINS
1855
OIL ON CARDBOARD
15⅝ × 21⅝"
COLLECTION NATIONAL GALLERY OF ART, WASHINGTON
PAUL MELLON COLLECTION

Born July 26, 1796, at Wilkes-Barre, Pennsylvania. Studied law and practiced briefly before beginning painting career in Philadelphia, 1823. Traveled 2,000 miles up Missouri River to Ft. Union, 1832; painted in Oklahoma and Arkansas Territories, 1835; in Minnesota in 1839. Toured his show, "Catlin's Indian Gallery," including performances, artifacts, and 507 paintings, in Great Britain and France, 1840-1852. Forced to sell the paintings in 1852 to pay debts. Traveled to Cuba, South America, Pacific Coast; crossed central Idaho mountains and returned to coast via Oregon Trail, 1855. Published Last Rambles Amongst the Indians of the Rocky Mountains and the Andes, *1867, describing this journey; discussed the Lost River Range and other Idaho geology in* Lifted and Subsided Rocks of America, *1870. Lived in Brussels, 1860-70, repainting Indian scenes. Died in Jersey City, New Jersey, in December, 1872.*

George Catlin was no longer a young man when he decided to journey to the Rocky Mountains in the mid-1850s. At age fifty-nine, he was a well-known artist whose Western scenes and portraits of Native Americans had been exhibited on the East Coast and in Europe. Moreover, he was an experienced artist-explorer who had made numerous excursions into frontier regions across the Trans-Mississippi West.

Catlin first visited Idaho's mountain country in 1855 following a trip to South America. He traveled north along the Pacific Coast and then headed toward Walla Walla, seeking provisions for his trek into the Rocky Mountains. He and his traveling companion, Caesar Bolla, an escaped slave from Havana, acquired "a horse and a couple of good mules" before continuing east by way of the Columbia and Snake Rivers. After five days' ride along the Snake, Catlin and Bolla climbed the difficult hillsides along the south bank of the Salmon River. Negotiating steep mountainous terrain for many days, they eventually reached the Salmon River Valley. Catlin wrote of his adventure, "The eighth day opened to our view one of the most verdant and beautiful valleys in the world; and on the tenth a distant smoke was observed, and under it the skin tents, which I at once recognized as of a Crow village."[1] Catlin had arrived at a summer encampment of Crow Indians whose teepees he would paint as he saw them set against the rugged Salmon River range.

Catlin recounts, "The Crow village that we were in, consisting of some forty or fifty skin tents, had crossed the mountains on to the head waters of the Salmon River, to take and dry salmon, there being no salmon on the east side of the Rocky Mountains."[2] After being kindly received, Catlin and his companion resumed their journey, traversing the Lost River region and continuing on to Fort Hall.

1. Catlin, George. *Episodes from* Life Among the Indians *and* Last Rambles Amongst the Indians of the Rocky Mountains and the Andes (Norman: University of Oklahoma, 1959) 147.
2. Catlin, 148.

JOHN MIX STANLEY

JOHN MIX STANLEY
ON THE SNAKE RIVER
CIRCA 1850
OIL ON CANVAS
36 × 54"
COURTESY KENNEDY GALLERIES, INC., NEW YORK

For more than a decade John Mix Stanley roamed the Western frontier documenting Native American life and recording the vast tract of plains, mountains, and rivers spanning from Mexico to the Pacific Northwest. He began painting Indian portraits at Fort Snelling, Minnesota, as early as 1839 and for six years stayed on the move before accompanying Colonel Stephen Kearny as topographic draftsman on his 1846 military march to California. In 1853 Stanley joined a second historic expedition, traveling with Isaac Stevens as an official artist on the Pacific Railroad Survey. During these trips, he was twice in Oregon and Washington territories, once at the conclusion of his work for Kearny and again with Stevens.

Stanley's landscapes, stemming from his western sojourns, were generally spectacular views observed on site and later reproduced from sketches at his eastern studio. While in the field, Stanley made precise descriptions in watercolor, which he later translated to canvas as oil paintings. Scenes like *On The Snake River* are idealized interpretations conveying the atmosphere and generalized idea of the country, rather than literally truthful renderings. He portrayed the land at its most dramatic, never showing the hardships caused by inclement weather and the struggles of frontier life.

If Stanley's efforts appear too idealized, one must recognize that his mission was to represent for an eastern political audience the bountiful country through which the northern railroad route to the Pacific was destined to pass. To fund such a venture, Congress needed to be persuaded that the Northwest was a worthwhile destination. Sublime images, such as those of John Mix Stanley, described the territories in a grand manner which effectively contributed to western expansion.

Born January 17, 1814, in Canandaigua, New York. Worked for a wagonmaster and as a house and sign painter in New York. Moved to Detroit in 1834 and learned portrait painting from James Bowman; opened a studio with him in Chicago and worked as an itinerant portrait painter on the East Coast, 1839-43. Painted Indian portraits and scenes on the southwestern frontier, 1839 and 1842-46. Joined Kearny's expedition to California, 1846, as draftsman. Traveled in Oregon, then to Hawaii, 1848. Exhibited his North American Indian Gallery in New York, 1850; moved it to the Smithsonian Institution in 1852; most works were destroyed by fire in 1865. Joined Pacific Railroad Survey in 1853, working as expedition artist from Ft. Benton to Vancouver. Returned to Washington, D.C., painted and toured large "Western Wilds" panorama. Moved to Buffalo in 1863, then Detroit in 1864, continuing to paint Western subjects. Died in Detroit, April 10, 1872.

GUSTAVUS SOHON

As a young man, Gustavus Sohon emigrated to the United States from his homeland in Germany. In 1852, after ten years working in New York City as a bookbinder and wood carver, he enlisted in the military and was assigned to go west as a topographical draftsman. Sohon worked initially in California before joining Lieutenant John Mullan's mission to develop a viable railroad route through the northern ranges of the Rockies. During the winter of 1853-54 with the Mullan party, he explored the difficult terrain of the Coeur d'Alene Mountains in what is now northern Idaho.

Sohon possessed a natural aptitude for languages, and his drawing abilities enabled him to converse easily with tribal members and learn their complex languages. As part of his duties, Sohon pictorially recorded numerous treaty negotiations which he attended as interpreter. His watercolor and pencil drawings touch on a variety of subjects including landscapes, portraits, and genre scenes of Indian life. Sohon also prepared maps, compiled meteorological data, and illustrated government reports of the expedition.

While on the west side of the Bitterroot Mountains, Sohon made renderings of the *Coeur d'Alene Mission of the Sacred Heart*, the settlement at the center of tribal activity in the area. He described in rich detail the mission structure and surrounding buildings, which were erected under the auspices of the Jesuits between 1848 and 1853. The restored church, now known as the Cataldo Mission, is the oldest surviving mission church in the Pacific Northwest, as well as the oldest standing structure in Idaho.

Born December 10, 1825, in Tilsit, East Prussia. Came to United States in 1842. Enlisted in the U.S. Army, 1852. Served in Isaac Stevens' Railroad Survey, working from the Pacific eastward to the Bitterroot Mountains, 1853-54. Assigned to Lt. John Mullan's party in Montana and Idaho. Interpreter and liaison for Stevens in 1855 Indian treaty negotiations; illustrated Stevens' survey report. In 1860-62, helped Lt. Mullan survey, construct, and document the Mullan Road from Ft. Benton to Ft. Walla Walla. Owned a photographic studio in San Francisco 1863-65 before returning to Washington, D.C. Died in Washington, September 3, 1903.

GUSTAVUS SOHON
COEUR D'ALENE MISSION IN THE ROCKY MOUNTAINS
1863
LITHOGRAPH
5 × 8½"
COLLECTION IDAHO STATE HISTORICAL SOCIETY LIBRARY AND ARCHIVES

Sohon worked in the Pacific Northwest for a decade. After his army service was completed, he continued as a civilian agent serving as interpreter for Mullan and monitoring the construction of the the military road Mullan had plotted from Ft. Benton to Walla Walla. In 1862, Sohon returned to Washington, D.C. to assist in the preparation of Lt. Mullan's military report. The original drawing of the *Coeur d'Alene Mission of the Sacred Heart* made by Sohon was translated to a lithograph and used to illustrate the published document.

Gustuvas Sohon never returned to the Rockies, and no artwork is known to exist after his departure from the West. He spent the last years of his life in relative obscurity, raising a large family and running a shoe business. However, Sohon made his mark in history by leaving over one hundred surviving sketches, termed "the most extensive pictorial series on Indians of the Northwestern Plateau in pre-reservation days."[1]

1. Ewers, John C. *Gustavus Sohon's Portraits of Flathead and Pend d'Oreille Indians, 1854* (Washington, D.C.: Smithsonian Institution, 1948) 13.

GUSTAVUS SOHON
NEZ PERCE ARRIVING AT
WALLA WALLA COUNCIL
1855
PENCIL ON PAPER
8 × 12"
COLLECTION NATIONAL ANTHROPOLOGICAL ARCHIVES
SMITHSONIAN INSTITUTION

JAMES MADISON ALDEN

JAMES MADISON ALDEN
SINYAKWATEEN DEPOT FROM NEAR LEFT BANK OF CLARKE'S FORK
CIRCA 1860
WATERCOLOR ON PAPER
9¾ × 13⅛"
COLLECTION NATIONAL ARCHIVES, WASHINGTON, D.C.

Born September 26, 1834, in Boxboro, Massachusetts. Joined the U.S. Coast Survey in 1853 under his uncle James Alden, Jr. Studied cartographic drawing in Washington, D.C., and in New York with Thomas Cummings. Went to San Francisco in 1854 to work as assistant to William McMurtrie, official artist of the Pacific Coast Survey. Appointed in 1857 to the Northwest Boundary Survey. Served as purser's steward in 1857, official artist during fieldwork from 1858 to 1860; worked in 1861 on Survey Report illustrations. Served in the Union Navy 1863-65 under Rear Admiral David Dixon Porter; worked as Porter's secretary after 1866, living in Washington, D.C. Moved to Florida in 1891 and died in Orlando in 1922.

James Madison Alden was one of the important artists who served during the Northwest exploration surveys. As a young man Alden was encouraged by his uncle, a naval officer, to take up a career in the military. Displaying an interest and talent in art, Alden studied cartographic drawing at the U. S. Coast Survey headquarters and aesthetic interpretation under Thomas Weir Cummings, the founder of the National Academy of Design.

Few topographical artists have been given such prestigious opportunities as James Alden when he was appointed to accompany the United States Pacific Coast Survey in 1854. On the journey he pictorially documented the coastline from San Diego to Puget Sound. Government officials, pleased with his precise renderings, requested his participation in the 1857 Northwest Boundary Survey to establish the demarcation line between Canada and the United States.

By the time Alden reached the Clark Fork area of Idaho in 1860, he had already spent more than five years in the field working along the Pacific coast and the forested terrain of what is now the Canadian border. Alden's background and expertise served him well as he recorded scenic landscapes, Indian life, pioneering progress, and early settlements. He portrayed what he saw in dramatic sweeping images and wide panoramas. He focused on relatively unspoiled natural settings, providing geological and topographic information needed by the Survey, enhanced by an artistic viewpoint. More than simply utilitarian drawings, Alden's vistas were sensitively composed works evoking a mood of quiet serenity.

The Civil War interrupted the final phases of the survey and much of the preliminary draft material was lost; the official Northwest Boundary Survey Report was never published. Alden remained virtually unknown as an artist, and it was not until an exhibition featuring his work at Fort Worth's Amon Carter Museum in 1975 that his drawings were publicly acclaimed.

ARM HINCELIN

ARM HINCELIN
MAIN STREET, BOISE
1864
OIL ON CANVAS
12 × 20"
COLLECTION IDAHO STATE HISTORICAL SOCIETY

Arm Hincelin, like other aspiring artists of his day, found the West a hard place to make a living, even for a versatile individual with a variety of marketable skills. While very little is known of his personal life, existing evidence indicates that Hincelin worked in Boise during the mid-nineteenth century. A jack-of-all-trades, he placed an advertisement in an August 1866 edition of Boise's *Tri-Weekly Statesman* offering his services as "House, Sign, and Ornamental Painter." His numerous talents included carriage painting, graining, gilding and paper hanging. In addition, he was willing to paint portraits and landscapes "executed in an artistic manner at moderate figures."

Hincelin's 1864 painting of Main Street is significant as the first known view of Boise. Naive in approach and execution, the painting depicts the wide expanse of Main Street lined with retail shops. Receding into the distance along the roof lines are the merchant signs: "City Brewery," "Oregon Tailor," "Tin Shop," "Livery and Feed Stable," "Chop House," and other storefront advertising which can be identified in detail under a magnifying glass. The townsfolk, going about their daily tasks, give a sense of life to this early Boise panorama.

INITIAL VISIONS

The dictates of topography primarily determined where the influx of population came into the Northwest territories. The easiest corridors through mountain passes became the principal routes. A natural gateway over the Continental Divide was situated through South Pass in the Rocky Mountains of Wyoming, allowing access to the Bear River Valley, Soda Springs and eventually across to Fort Hall. A number of early immigrants came by way of this South Pass route into Idaho, ultimately traveling on to either Oregon or California. The trickle became a flood, and the trail west along the Snake River through Idaho became a clearly defined section of the Oregon Trail.

When gold and silver were discovered in the north and central mountains of what is now Idaho in the 1860s, a surge of fortune seekers poured into the region. News spread quickly and thousands of individuals with get-rich-quick attitudes came to exploit the extensive mineral resources. On the whole, these prospectors were a young, independent breed who moved from camp to camp in search of wealth, traversing the region from the Coeur d'Alenes in the north, to Boise Basin and the Sawtooths in the central mountains, and to the Owyhees in the south. A small number of artists found their subject matter in the mining camps, and even though many artworks dating from the mid-nineteenth century have an amateur quality, they are important documents of western history.

The need for a transportation link with the West Coast, especially in light of the discovery of gold in California, spurred the building of transcontinental railroads. As a result of the search for a feasible northern railroad route, the Mullan Road was opened as an artery from the east through the Bitterroot Basin into what is presently Idaho's northern panhandle. With the success of Idaho mining ventures and the arrival of the railroads, boomtowns grew up as a torrent of outsiders arrived to begin a new life.

While the railroad helped opened access to north Idaho, and the Oregon Trail served the south, the rugged central mountains still made travel difficult between these two sections of the state. Steep mountains and river canyons, transecting the central portion of the territory, forbade passage to all but those hardy individuals willing to tackle the rough terrain by foot or on horseback. Some of these were itinerant artists who, beginning in the 1880s, crisscrossed the state to make their livelihood. These roving artists depicted mines, farms, communities, homes, and early businesses in exchange for a meager living which often amounted to only room and board. Some artists received commissions, but most found it hard to eke out a living. Those with sufficient artistic talent often turned to more practical trades like carriage painting or sign making.

How the territory and state were viewed by outsiders during the late eighteen-hundreds was greatly influenced by artists who came into the Pacific Northwest to depict the natural resources and business opportunities of the area. Commissioned by speculators, promoters, and railroad developers, their job was to attract immigrants and investors by portraying Northwest communities in a favorable light. Illustrators like Augustus Koch and W. W. Elliott produced urban and rural scenes for these commercial purposes. At that time, most publishers used lithography to transform artists' drawings to printed material. Civic leaders, often subsidizing publications to make larger distribution possible, used these views to attract residents and business investment to their communities.

Magazine illustrators were another group of artists who portrayed exciting visions of the Northwest. Their drawings, which primarily dealt with adventure subjects and social drama, accompanied feature stories for popular eastern publications. Periodicals such as *Frank Leslie's Illustrated Newspaper* and *Harper's Weekly* employed many artist-correspondents to represent frontier life as they witnessed it on the western plains.

Beginning in the 1880s, many viewmakers increasingly relied on the camera for their images. While photographers like Frank Jay Haynes, Frank Palmer, Thomas Barnard and Nellie Stockbridge promoted commercial interests in the Northwest at the turn of the century, their pictures of life in the panhandle region now give us an important record of settlement days.

Women played an important, if unsung, role in producing early wilderness landscapes and western subjects. Their works are lesser known because they did not serve as official expedition artists with government surveys, nor were they among the itinerant artists who sought employment as they traveled the state. Most came to Idaho as wives or family members, although a few came seeking employment opportunities. Usually, the more accomplished women artists who came to the mining camps and early towns had been educated in eastern art schools. Often they were particularly independent individuals, supportive of suffragette causes and prohibition. Upon arrival, many became teachers and art instructors who promoted the development of local cultural amenities and the arts in their new communities.

When professional artists like Thomas Moran and James Everett Stuart came west before the turn of the century, their route through the region usually included a stop at Shoshone Falls, one of southern Idaho's widely known and most remarkable landmarks. In their time, the great painting of Niagara Falls by Frederic Church, which had been executed in 1857, was well-known and celebrated in eastern art circles. Some artists felt that Shoshone Falls, which was forty-five feet higher, rivaled Niagara Falls as subject matter in both splendor and grandeur. The most famous image of Shoshone Falls, eleven feet in length and currently housed in Oklahoma's Gilcrease Museum, was executed by Thomas Moran in 1900 and is the epitome of the romantic and sublime in western art.

THOMAS MORAN
SHOSHONE FALLS ON SNAKE RIVER
1900
OIL ON CANVAS
52 × 132"
COURTESY THE THOMAS GILCREASE INSTITUTE OF AMERICAN HISTORY AND ART, TULSA, OKLAHOMA

MARGARETTA FAVORITE BROWN

Mining was the magnet that attracted a wave of young men west, and with them came adventurous and hardy women. A pioneer Idaho City artist of note was Maggie F. Brown, who lived in the community from 1864 to 1882 at the height of the Idaho gold rush. Originally from Missouri, Maggie Brown went to California to join her sister sometime before 1857. There she married self-taught lawyer Jonas Brown. Like many adventurers ready to find fortune, the couple came to work in the placer mines of Boise Basin.

Idaho City was a town of contrasts, comprised of prospectors, Confederate refugees, and outlaws as well as a local contingent of churchgoers and upstanding citizens. It was said that in Idaho City "the priest and the saloon-keeper jostle each other on the sidewalks, and the gentleman's wife must walk around the trail of the courtesan who lives next door."[1]

Margaretta Brown was an active member of the Good Templars, an organization whose main aim was to promote sobriety. She is best known for her moralistic murals of Faith, The Good Samaritan, and Hope produced for the walls of The Good Templars' Hall. These paintings were created in the hope that their somber influence would encourage temperance. It is thus ironic that Maggie Brown, the active prohibitionist, often auctioned her artwork in Idaho City saloons.

A variety of subject matter attracted Margaretta's interest, including town figures, miners, and merchants as well as landscapes and scenes from daily life. *Hydraulic Mining in the Boise Basin* is a detailed view of an active mining claim which is thought to be East Hill or Gold Hill near Idaho City. In this image of a large-scale hydraulic mine, she shows the process in which miners direct tremendous sprays of water into the gold-bearing hillside. Unlike many of her works in dark tones, this painting, executed in a flat style, has a chalky muted surface. One story suggests that she learned to mix pigments from Indians in California and that the homemade colors account for her limited color palette.

Margaretta Brown, who died in 1897, is honored as an important pioneer artist whose work offers an historical record of life in a Boise Basin community.

1. *Idaho; An Illustrated History* (Boise: Idaho State Historical Society, 1976) 41.

Born in McConnellsville, Pennsylvania, on July 31, 1818. Married Jonas W. Brown, a lawyer and gold miner, in Yreka, California, in 1857. Moved with him to Portland, then to Idaho City in 1864. Moved to Boise in 1882. Died November 2, 1897, and is buried in the Pioneer Cemetery in Boise. Works located in Idaho City Masonic Temple and Odd Fellows Hall, Idaho Historical Museum. Her painting Hydraulic Mining in the Boise Basin *was included in the exhibitions* Northwest History in Art *(Washington State Historical Society, 1963) and* Artists in Aprons: Folk Art by American Women *(Museum of American Folk Art, N.Y., 1979).*

MARGARETTA FAVORITE BROWN
HYDRAULIC MINING IN BOISE BASIN
CIRCA 1870-80
OIL ON CANVAS
26½ × 20¾"
COLLECTION IDAHO STATE HISTORICAL SOCIETY

PETER MORAN

PETER MORAN
THE TETONS
1879
WATERCOLOR ON PAPER
12 × 18"
COLLECTION ROSWELL MUSEUM & ART CENTER
GIFT OF SENATOR CLINTON P. ANDERSON

Born at Bolton, Lancashire, England, on March 4, 1841. Came to the United States in 1844. Apprenticed briefly to a lithographer at the age of 16; studied art with his brothers Thomas and Edward. Specialized in animal painting; went to England in 1863 to study the work of Edwin Landseer. Opened a studio in Philadelphia in 1864. Traveled several times to the West, including a trip to the Grand Tetons in 1879 with Thomas Moran. Worked in New Mexico and Arizona between 1880 and 1883; in Wyoming in 1890. Died in Philadelphia, November 9, 1914. President of Philadelphia Society of Etchers; exhibited etchings at the Centennial Exposition, 1876, and the Boston Art Museum, 1881; member of various artistic associations, from whom he received many honors.

In 1879, two brothers, Thomas and Peter Moran, headed west to a destination in the Teton Mountains on a venture commissioned by the Union Pacific Railroad. At forty-two and thirty-eight respectively, the Morans were mature artists whose images of the West reflected the sublime in nature and offered a romantic realist viewpoint.

As children, Thomas and Peter Moran received art instruction from their older brother Edward. They each apprenticed with artisans in Philadelphia, and both traveled to England to further their artistic studies. In Europe, Peter Moran was influenced by the animal paintings of Edwin Landseer and Rosa Bonheur. He became interested in portraying animal life and focused on this theme during his lifetime. On the other hand, Thomas Moran was charged with inspiration after seeing William Turner's windswept landscapes, work which affected him throughout his career.

In 1864, Peter Moran made his first trip to the western United States. Upon Thomas Moran's return from England in 1871, he too joined an expedition to the wilderness of the Far West. Though both brothers produced work directly from their western experiences, Thomas Moran's paintings were considered more significant. Based on his travels, he painted large panoramic views including *The Grand Canyon of the Yellowstone* and *Chasm of the Colorado*, both of which were purchased by Congress and installed in the Capitol building in Washington, D.C. They were considered among the finest "pictorial records of the stupendous scenery of still unfamiliar regions."[1] Thus by the time the Union Pacific Railroad commissioned Thomas Moran, and Peter had agreed to accompany him, the brothers were already well-regarded artists with successful careers.

In addition to the commission from the Union Pacific, Thomas Moran had an ulterior motive for coming to the Rocky Mountains which border Idaho and Wyoming. In 1872, F. V. Hayden had named Mount Moran, the most impressive peak of the three Tetons, in

THOMAS MORAN
THE TETONS, IDAHO
1879
INK WASH ON PAPER
14 × 10"
COLLECTION NATIONAL PARK SERVICE
GRAND TETON NATIONAL PARK

honor of the artist. Moran had originally planned to visit the Tetons with Hayden's geological expedition in 1873. However, his plans changed and he was unable to go. It became Moran's ambition to see and paint this namesake peak.

As recorded in Thomas Moran's journal, the brothers spent most of August 1879 in Nevada, Utah, and eastern Idaho. Toward the end of August they arrived at Fort Hall, where a military escort was retained to guide them on a twelve-day ride into the Tetons. After leaving Fort Hall, Moran noted "the difficult conditions of the trip through potentially hostile Indian country that was dry, dusty, windy and rife with fires."[2]

On approaching the Tetons he wrote, "The distant range is of an exquisite blue with but little definition of forms on their surfaces."[3] On reaching the Teton Basin, Moran notes, "The Tetons here loomed up grandly against the sky and from this point it is perhaps the finest pictorial range in the United States or even in N. America."[4]

In the late summer of 1879, Thomas and Peter Moran both sketched watercolor versions of the Teton range. But Thomas, more than Peter, is remembered for the landscapes he painted of southern Idaho. His fresh, fluid watercolors of the mountain range inspired his oil painting *The Three Tetons*, a canvas which now hangs in the Oval Office of the White House. Thomas Moran's most famous image, one also generated by seeing a southern Idaho landmark, is a spectacular eleven-foot-long painting of *Shoshone Falls* which is currently in the Thomas Gilcrease Institute of American History and Art in Tulsa, Oklahoma.

Fortunately for the art world and those who have a high regard for the pristine beauty of the western landscape, Thomas and Peter Moran were prolific artists who left an astonishing body of work documenting the American West.

1. *Dictionary of American Biography*, vol. 13 (N.Y.: Scribners, 1934) 153.
2. Fryxell, Fritiof M. "Thomas Moran's Journey to the Tetons in 1879." *Augustana Historical Society Publications* no.2(1932):3-12.
3. Fryxell, Moran's 1879 diary entry for August 23, Grand Teton National Park.
4. Fryxell, entry for August 25.

Born January 12, 1837, at Bolton, Lancashire, England. Moved to United States with his family; settled in Philadelphia, 1845. Apprenticed to a lithographer, then began painting and etching in 1850s. Taught in Philadelphia and traveled in Britain and Europe in the 1860s. Married Mary Nimmo, of Scotland, in 1862. Made his first trip West in 1871 with the Hayden Survey in Montana; returned to Utah, California, and Wyoming, 1872-74. Traveled in 1879 to Grand Tetons, then to California and back through southern Idaho. Toured Colorado, the Southwest, and Mexico repeatedly in the 1880s and 1890s; visited southern Idaho during his travels in 1900. Continued to work in Europe, the East Coast, and the Western states; after 1916 he spent summers in East Hampton, N.Y. and winters in California, taking sketching trips especially to the Grand Canyon. Died on August 25, 1925, in Santa Barbara, California.

CHARLES LEOPOLD OSTNER

Travelers came to America from Europe for a host of different reasons. For some the voyage was taken for sheer adventure; for others like Charles Ostner, it was politically motivated. Ostner, who was a resident of Heidelberg, Germany, left his native land to escape persecution after becoming involved in the German student uprisings of 1848.

Like so many other young immigrants during the westward expansion, Ostner could not resist the allure of the gold fields. He followed the mining fever and prospected at sites in northern California and Canada. From there, the news of rich new claims in Idaho enticed him to leave for the Florence mining district in 1860. The trip was a difficult and unsuccessful experience. On the way to the gold fields, he was lost in mountainous terrain for nearly thirty days. When discovered, he was very ill, emaciated, and unconscious. Ostner recuperated but did not choose to continue life as a prospector.

Failing to strike it rich, Ostner set out to pursue a more profitable enterprise. He settled in the rugged area on the south fork of the Payette River and purchased interest in a pack-trail bridge at Garden Valley. This toll-bridge was situated on a route through the Salmon River Basin from the Placerville area to mines in north Idaho.

Born in Baden, Austria, in 1828. Studied at the University of Heidelberg. Immigrated to the United States in 1848. Lived in Philadelphia and New Orleans; settled in San Francisco, 1850. Prospected for gold in California; headed for Florence, Idaho in 1860. Homesteaded in Garden Valley, 1864; moved to Boise in 1869. Traveled extensively in Europe, Central America, Canada and Alaska. Died in Boise December 6, 1913. Artistic activities included painting, drawing for lithographic views, stone-carving for buildings and tombstones. Sculpted a seven-foot-high equestrian statue of George Washington, carved of wood and painted bronze. Statue presented to 1869 Territorial Legislature is now covered with gold leaf and displayed in the State Capitol Building.

CHARLES OSTNER
LEAVING FOR DEADWOOD
CIRCA 1865
OIL ON CANVAS
26⅝ × 33⅝"
COLLECTION IDAHO STATE HISTORICAL SOCIETY

Ostner's Garden Valley home served as the setting for his painting *Leaving for Deadwood*. Here Ostner portrays three prospectors readying their packs for a trip up to the mines. His European art training is evident in the staged elliptical format in which the lines of each figure lead the eye from one form to the other. He also reveals his northern European artistic background by simplifying forms and rendering them in somber colors. The charm of this work lies in his naive, stylized interpretation of these robust figures.

In Ostner's painting *Bear's Attack*, the elaborately garbed Indian astride his rearing white horse valiantly battles a grizzly. This painting, like nearly all Ostner's known artwork, uses the horse as a primary focus. The artist dramatizes his romantic view of the struggle, framing the scene with trees and bushes and highlighting the central action with diagonal lines. Like most western artists in the 1800s, Ostner presented an idealized version of reality.

CHARLES OSTNER
BEAR'S ATTACK
CIRCA 1865
OIL ON CANVAS
26⅛ × 33⅞"
COLLECTION IDAHO STATE HISTORICAL SOCIETY

EDMOND GREENE

EDMOND GREENE
SHOSHONE TWIN FALLS OF SNAKE RIVER
CIRCA 1880
LITHOGRAPH BY HENRY STEINEGGER
14¼ x 20"
COLLECTION IDAHO STATE HISTORICAL SOCIETY

Born in England around 1830. Traveled throughout southern Idaho between 1879 and 1884. Many of his sketches were redrawn by lithographer Henry Steinegger for the San Francisco publishers Britton & Rey.

What we know of Idaho in its frontier years is greatly enhanced by the highly detailed views of early towns produced by itinerant artists. Between 1879 and 1884 Edmond Greene made it his business to document mountains, scenic sites, mining districts and boom towns of southern Idaho.

Edmond Greene was recognized in his day and mentioned in several articles of the *Tri-Weekly Statesman* in the 1880s. One excerpt recounts his trip to Alturas County: "He has recently visited and sketched in crayon the Great Shoshone falls and Twin falls on Snake river....When lithographed, these views will form splendid pictures....His sketches of Snake river scenery cannot be surpassed in beauty of execution and fidelity to nature."[1]

Commercial artists such as Edmond Greene sought to sell advance subscriptions to finance reproduction of their drawings. An 1884 *Statesman* article describes the process. First Greene's image was exhibited in a local store; then he set forth on "a tour of the city and adjacent country...for the purpose of affording all an opportunity to subscribe for a copy of the picture."[2] A guarantee of 100 impressions at $3 each made it economically feasible for him to have a print professionally executed.

To accomplish the final task, Greene sent original drawings to lithographers in San Francisco, where the image was redrawn directly on the surface of a smooth stone plate with a greasy "tusche ink" or litho crayon. The grease crayon permitted the lithographer to scratch in textures with sandpaper or needles to achieve detail; tones were created by soft crayons as they are in drawing. The result was a high-quality, clearly defined reproduction of the original.

Although little is known of Edmond Greene personally, his renderings of Atlanta, Shoshone Falls, Bonanza City, Quartzburg, Garden Valley, and other sites remain an important pictorial record of pioneer Idaho.

1. *Tri-Weekly Statesman* [Boise] 30 Sept. 1879: 3.
2. *Statesman* [Boise] 8 July 1884: 3.

WILLIAM HENRY JACKSON

WILLIAM HENRY JACKSON
FORT HALL, IDAHO
CIRCA 1930
WATERCOLOR ON PAPER
9½ x 14¼"
COLLECTION BUFFALO BILL HISTORICAL CENTER
CODY, WYOMING

Few artists saw the transformation of the West over such an extensive period of time as William Henry Jackson. In a career spanning over seventy-five years, Jackson produced documentary photographs and descriptive paintings which, in addition to their aesthetic merits, have become important records of the territorial West.

In 1866, when Jackson first traversed the Oregon Trail on a wagon train, he sketched historical landmarks and frontier settlements, subject matter which later in life would provide material for his paintings. After 1868 Jackson traveled widely, photographing Indians, frontiersmen, and the construction of the transcontinental railroad. Then, in 1871, he became the official photographer for the Hayden Geological Survey expedition, and for the following eight summers he photographed frontier development. When the Survey was discontinued in 1879, it was Jackson's images along with the dramatic paintings of Thomas Moran, who also accompanied the expedition, that helped persuade Congress to create Yellowstone National Park.

During the 1930s, when Oregon Trail Association president Howard Driggs — descendent of Driggs, Idaho pioneers — was looking for an artist to illustrate a book about the historic Oregon route, he wanted to commission an individual who had witnessed firsthand the migration west. The appropriate choice was William Henry Jackson. Although Jackson, then in his eighties, was one of the most famous western photographers, he was also a painter of considerable talent. For the Oregon Trail Association, Jackson was commissioned to illustrate their new edition of historian Francis Parkman's account of his 1846 passage west. Jackson's paintings reconstruct points of interest along the immigrant trail as they might have appeared to Parkman in the mid-nineteenth century. His watercolor of Fort Hall, detailing the arrival of settlers, is executed in a vibrant narrative painting style.

Born April 4, 1843, in Keeseville, New York. Worked at age 15 as a photographic retouching artist. Served in the Civil War 1862-1863. Traveled West in 1866, opened Jackson Brothers' Photography Studio in Omaha in 1867, specializing in Indian portraits and landscape studies. Official member of F. V. Hayden's U.S. Geological Survey of the Territories; photographed Yellowstone region, Colorado, and Rocky Mountains, 1871-1878. Operated a commercial studio in Denver 1879-1895; took photographs for Santa Fe and B&O Railroads, World's Columbian Exposition of 1893, and abroad for World's Transportation Commission. Worked for Detroit Photographic Company, a mass-marked postcard and "view" company, from 1897 until its bankruptcy in 1924. Moved to Washington, D.C., in 1924, then New York in 1929 to work for the Oregon Trail Memorial Association. Painted murals of Hayden Surveys for WPA and paintings for National Park Service, 1936-37. Published his autobiography, Time Exposures, *in 1940. Died in New York City, June 30, 1942.*

FRANK LESLIE'S ILLUSTRATED NEWSPAPER

FRANK LESLIE'S ILLUSTRATED NEWSPAPER

No. 1,491.—Vol. LVIII.] NEW YORK—FOR THE WEEK ENDING APRIL 19, 1884. [Price, 10 Cents.

OUR ARTIST'S WANDERINGS IN THE FAR WEST.—THE FIRST WOMAN IN CAMP IN THE CŒUR D'ALENE MINING DISTRICT, IDAHO.

FRANK LESLIE'S ILLUSTRATED NEWSPAPER
THE FIRST WOMAN IN CAMP IN THE COEUR D'ALENE MINING DISTRICT, IDAHO
WEEK ENDING APRIL 19, 1884, COVER PAGE
LITHOGRAPH
$15\frac{1}{2} \times 10\frac{7}{8}$"
COLLECTION IDAHO STATE HISTORICAL SOCIETY LIBRARY AND ARCHIVES

The news and excitement that sold eastern newspapers during the time of the Civil War came from the Confederate South. In the post-war years, however, the source of popular-interest stories shifted to the West. Two leading eastern pictorial magazines, *Harper's Weekly* and *Frank Leslie's Illustrated Newspaper*, influenced the way the world envisioned Idaho and the American Far West during the last quarter of the nineteenth century.

With the completion of the transcontinental railroad in 1869, Frank Leslie, a New York publisher, capitalized on an idea to send artist-reporters to the frontier territories. His intent was to hire journalists to send back cover illustrations and descriptive essays for a weekly periodical. Immediately popular, this magazine's appeal was the on-the-spot record of distant events and the triumphs and struggles of real-life people.

HARPER'S WEEKLY.

A JOURNAL OF CIVILIZATION.

Vol. XXI.—No. 1083.] NEW YORK, SATURDAY, SEPTEMBER 29, 1877. [WITH A SUPPLEMENT. PRICE TEN CENTS.

Entered according to Act of Congress, in the Year 1877, by Harper & Brothers, in the Office of the Librarian of Congress, at Washington.

DEAD MULE TRAIL, IDAHO.—From a Sketch by an Army Officer.—[See Page 765.]

HARPER'S WEEKLY
DEAD MULE TRAIL, FROM A SKETCH BY AN ARMY OFFICER
SEPTEMBER 29, 1877, COVER PAGE
LITHOGRAPH
$15^3/_8 \times 10^7/_8$"
COLLECTION IDAHO STATE HISTORICAL SOCIETY
LIBRARY AND ARCHIVES

In 1873, in order to compete with Frank Leslie's successful journal, *Harper's Weekly* proposed to give readers a "fresh view" of life in the West. Its artists were encouraged to venture away from the railroad lines to record incidents off the regularly traveled routes.

In contrast to earlier documentary accounts produced by pioneers, survey agents, or the military, these two periodicals were meant to inspire the reader's imagination and to tell graphic stories rather than just describe factual events. In a report on Idaho, *Frank Leslie's Illustrated Newspaper* offers a highly sentimental version of the arrival of the first woman at camp in the Coeur d'Alene mining district. A *Harper's Weekly* cover of 1877 depicts the exaggerated perils of Dead Mule Trail in mountainous Idaho. For the general public, flamboyant characters and thrilling narratives were often more appealing than skillfully rendered art.

AGNES BOWEN RICHTER

AGNES BOWEN RICHTER
WALTER'S FERRY ON SNAKE RIVER
1890
OIL ON CANVAS
10¼ × 18"
COLLECTION IDAHO STATE HISTORICAL SOCIETY

"It is doubtful whether any state in the nation has used as many ferries in its development as Idaho."[1] For the thousands of immigrants and settlers who made their way across the treacherous passes of the Rocky Mountains, the rivers of Idaho—primarily the Snake—were additional obstacles to negotiate. Most ferries served immigrants on their way to Oregon and many were used by miners en route to the gold camps of north Idaho and Montana. For the seventy years after 1850 more than 120 Idaho ferries facilitated travel and improved access to the West.

A ferryboat is a flatboat or scow which is drawn across a stream by means of oars and poles or by ropes and cables. Typical was Payne's Ferry, located on the Snake River two miles above Thousand Springs, on the route between Boise City and Brigham City. The painting of Payne's Ferry attributed to M. E. Black was actually created by a wandering landscape artist known as Sam Sleeper. According to a Payne family

MARY ELIZABETH BLACK

MARY ELIZABETH BLACK
PAYNE'S FERRY, IDAHO
1877
OIL ON CANVAS
23½ × 35½"
COLLECTION IDAHO STATE HISTORICAL SOCIETY

relative, Sleeper remained at the ferry for two weeks to complete the picture. The story goes that one of the girls from nearby Blacks Creek, who had taken art lessons in San Francisco, later took an interest in the painting. "She asked the Paynes to let her take the picture and touch it up and finish it in better shape, as Sleeper left it in rather crude form. I don't remember whether she had the picture while she was Miss Black or after she became Mrs. William Ridenbaugh. The original painter was Sleeper."[2]

As with many pioneer artists, little is known of Agnes Bowen Richter, painter of *Walter's Ferry*. Although she was a competent artist working in the style of the period, her vision of Walter's Ferry is primarily significant as a firsthand account of this early Idaho historical site. Walter's Ferry on the Snake River was the most direct means of access between the Boise Basin and the Owyhee mining camps of Silver City and the southern trails to Nevada and California. Ferryboats on the Snake encouraged settlement on both sides of the river, furnished transport of supplies to the miners, and helped develop Idaho's industries of ranching and farming.

Born in Harrison County, Missouri, October 10, 1857. At age seven, came to Idaho by covered wagon; her family ranched on the Wood River near Ketchum and ran a stage ferry. Studied at St. Michael's Parish School and at St. Vincent's College, Walla Walla. Taught school in Ada County. Married William Ridenbaugh, 1878. Served on innumerable public service boards, including three terms on University of Idaho Board of Regents, promoting study for women. Chairman of Idaho Board of World's Columbian Exposition in Chicago, 1893; hostess of Idaho building at Panama-Pacific Exposition in San Francisco, 1916. Died in Portland, Oregon, March 26, 1926.

1. Huntley, James L. *Ferry Boats in Idaho* (Caldwell, Idaho: Caxton Printers, 1979) 19.
2. Huntley 81.

ELLA KNOX PARRISH

Born July 11, 1868, near Boise. Moved to Emmett as a child. Married William Parrish on January 1, 1888. Honored during Territorial Centennial, 1963, as oldest native-born resident of the Emmett area. Died October 6, 1964.

Ella Knox Parrish, one of the few native pioneer artists of Idaho, was born in the Dry Creek area northwest of Boise in 1868. Her father, a well-known Ada County official, homesteaded and built the Knox family ranch near Emmett. As a young man Douglas Knox accompanied a train of ox-drawn wagons carrying milling equipment from Nebraska destined for the mines at Rocky Bar, Idaho. He remained in the central Idaho mountains and tried his hand at prospecting for several years in Rocky Bar and the Idaho City area, before deciding that the life of a miner was not his calling.

In the fall of 1866 Knox came to Boise Valley and worked at Dry Creek for a rancher who built a stage road through the Willow Creek hills. He married the rancher's daughter and eventually moved to Payette Valley, where he homesteaded three miles west of Emmett around 1870. Ella Knox Parrish was the eldest of Knox's eight children. When her mother died in 1887 she assumed the role of homemaker for the family. At eighteen she taught school for a year in Emmett before marrying William Parrish and raising a large family of her own. An active woman, she was involved in the Idaho Pioneer Society, Women's Christian Temperance Union, and the state Democratic Party.

The painting of Knox ranch is attributed to Ella Parrish. The overview of the house and surrounding outbuildings is painted in a style much like the popular views done by itinerant artists who toured the countryside documenting the appearance of homes, farms, and property. The perceptive interpretation of ranch life shows abundant gardens with plotted furrows bordered by an orchard. Although the style is naive, the artist demonstrates a familiarity with linear perspective. Delicate brush strokes detail the activity of rural nineteenth-century life in the Payette Valley.

ELLA PARRISH
PIONEER HOME OF DOUGLAS KNOX AND FAMILY, 1872
1883
OIL ON CANVAS
24 × 36"
COLLECTION IDAHO STATE HISTORICAL SOCIETY

WALLACE W. ELLIOTT

One of the earliest books describing Idaho is W. W. Elliott's *History of Idaho Territory*, published in San Francisco in 1884. The book is important because it offers a comprehensive history of Idaho's development with illustrations that detail many settlements and buildings, some of which are no longer in existence or for which no photographic records survive.

In the early 1880s, photographs could not yet be duplicated by the printing process. Thus it was an ambitious effort to organize a book accurately portraying numerous locations in a vast geographic area such as Idaho. Artists sometimes trekked through inhospitable terrain to record an image. Because they were under pressure to produce large quantities of work in a short time, their pictures often were quickly executed pencil sketches. When the publishers received the original drawings, they were translated to lithographs or engravings. The expertise of the lithographer was crucial in capturing the essence of the original sketch. What is most striking in the Elliott publication is how the finished prints convey the appearance of pencil drawings.

Scenic wonders, ranches, mines, local businesses, residences, mills, and hotels are Elliott's primary subjects. These images were intended to encourage settlers and promote investments in the region. Typical of such lithographs is the L. P. *Brown Lumber and Flour Mills and Mt. Idaho Ranch* near Florence. In Elliott's history, L. P. Brown is mentioned as a miller who first settled in Idaho County in 1862. Shown here after more than twenty years in the area, Brown's Mill appears to be prosperous. Quaintly rendered, the lithograph shows in detail the origins of lumber milling in Idaho County.

W. W. ELLIOTT
LUMBER AND FLOUR MILLS, &
MT. IDAHO RANCH
1884
LITHOGRAPH
8³/₈ × 11½"
COURTESY CAROLYN STALEY FINE PRINTS
SEATTLE, WASHINGTON

U. L. GRAY

U. L. GRAY
PACKER JOHN'S CABIN
CIRCA 1910
OIL ON CANVAS
19⅞ × 27½"
COLLECTION IDAHO STATE HISTORICAL SOCIETY

U. L. Gray worked as an itinerant painter in Idaho around 1910. He lived for a year or two in Boise's Idanha Hotel, and his only income reportedly came from his artwork. Little is known of U. L. Gray, but the subject of his painting, *Packer John's Cabin*, holds historic significance for Idahoans as the meeting place of the first territorial Democratic convention.

John Welch, popularly called Packer John, was a Lewiston miner who is said to have forged the trail that opened up Boise Basin to northern prospectors during the early days of Idaho's gold rush. In 1862, Welch constructed a rustic log cabin near present New Meadows in Adams County, as a storehouse for his emergency winter cache, halfway from Lewiston to the mines in Pioneerville.

When William Wallace, the newly appointed first governor of Idaho Territory, issued a proclamation calling for the election of legislators and a delegate to Congress, the Democratic factions chose to convene their first meeting at Packer John's cabin. The site was selected because it was part way between Boise Basin, where gold mining was in full swing, and Lewiston, the center of political activity in northern Idaho. U. L. Gray's painting of the historic meeting place pays tribute to John Welch, one of Idaho's earliest citizens, and the part that his cabin played in Idaho political annals.

EDWARD SMITH

EDWARD SMITH
SEVEN DEVILS MOUNTAINS
1893
OIL ON CANVAS
41¼ × 53¼"
COLLECTION IDAHO STATE HISTORICAL SOCIETY

The painting of *Seven Devils Mountains* is signed by Ed Smith. Although it is not a positive attribution, we believe the artist lived southeast of Whitebird, Idaho, and was one of the major stockmen and farmers of the area. Edward C. Smith crossed the plains with his parents in 1870 and lived in California, as well as Washington, before coming to homestead along the Salmon River in 1893. A well-educated man, he followed his father's vocation of farming and became a prosperous cattleman of Idaho County.

Born December 15, 1868, in Quincy, Illinois; emigrated to Sonoma County, California in 1870 and to Whitman County, Washington, in 1885. Attended school to age 18. Came to Idaho in 1893; married Esther Karnes, 1895.

FREDERIC REMINGTON

Register Rock, attributed to Frederic Remington, depicts one of Idaho's best-known landmarks on the Oregon Trail. Painted in 1891, the canvas shows the twenty-foot-high boulder located along the Snake River at a pioneer campsite southwest of American Falls, Idaho. Plainly evident in Remington's painting are immigrants' names, dates, and autographs, which are still visible on the massive rock today.

Frederic Remington, an Easterner by birth, became interested in recording the West during a sojourn in Montana in 1880. As a young man of nineteen, he traveled with a wagon freighter, sketching sights along the way. Sharing the campfires and reminiscences of trail hands, he came to realize that a colorful era was passing and decided to make it his vocation to portray the western landscape before it changed forever.

An avowed realist, Remington was faithful to the narrative tradition in art, and for the most part his paintings tell a story. He maintained authenticity by describing Native Americans in their appropriate tribal garments, rather than in generic Indian dress. Remington distinguished between types of horses, which differed from tribe to tribe as well, carefully noting details of the animals' appearance. To dramatize his scenes, he simplified the composition and used atmospheric effects such as blinding sun or blowing rain. In *Register Rock*, Remington reduced the tonal values and brightened the image to give it a heightened sense of realism.

By the time Remington painted *Register Rock* in 1891, he was already a successful illustrator in New York. His drawings appeared on the covers of *Harper's Weekly* and *Century Magazine* and he had produced illustrations for several successful books. He continued to return to the West into the 1890s, gathering background material for his work. Living a strenuous life in cowcamps and army barracks, he absorbed the atmosphere and tales of plains life. During his career, Remington fulfilled his commitment to document the vanishing frontier, and by 1895 was regarded as the foremost exponent of the Western scene.

Born October 4, 1861, in Canton, New York. Studied art at Yale University, 1878-80. Visited Montana in 1881, then worked in Albany at clerical jobs. Ran a Kansas sheep ranch, traveled through Southwest and Mexico, and returned to study at Art Students League in 1886. Produced hundreds of illustrations for 142 books and for 41 periodicals, based on travels in Europe, North Africa, Cuba, Mexico and the American Southwest and Northwest. Painted for private commissions; exhibited at National Academy of Design beginning in 1887. In 1895, produced the first of 25 bronze sculptures. Contracted with Collier's Weekly *in 1903 for a series of paintings of the frontier. Developed a new impressionistic style and created many landscape works before his death in Ridgefield, Connecticut, December 26, 1909.*

FREDERIC REMINGTON
REGISTER ROCK, IDAHO
ATTRIBUTED TO FREDERIC REMINGTON
1891
OIL ON CANVAS
17⅛ × 27¾
COLLECTION AMON CARTER MUSEUM, FORT WORTH

FRANK TENNEY JOHNSON

Born June 28, 1874, in Big Grove, Iowa. Educated in Wisconsin; studied art in Milwaukee with F. W. Heine and Richard Lorenz. Studied at Art Students League, 1902, and New York School of Art. Settled on a Colorado ranch in 1904 and began successful career as western illustrator. Moved to California in 1920 and opened a studio with Clyde Forsythe in Alhambra. Founded Biltmore Art Gallery in Los Angeles with Forsythe. Received many awards; work in collection of National Gallery and many museums across the country. Died in Los Angeles, January 1, 1939.

Raised on a ranch along the banks of the Missouri river, Frank Tenney Johnson witnessed migrations westward of frontiersmen and homesteaders. From the outset, these adventurous characters piqued his desire to portray Indians, cowboys, and settlers. He was further encouraged by one of his first instructors, artist and former Texas Ranger Frank Lorenz, who shared with Johnson his insights into the character and traits of cowpunchers, lawmen, and sodbusters.

Johnson's formal education was furthered under the tutelage of Robert Henri, William Merritt Chase and Kenneth Hayes Miller at the Art Students League in New York City. While Johnson first gained recognition in New York, he felt compelled to head west to see firsthand the cowboys and cattle he liked to paint. Early in his career, shortly after a move to Colorado, he sketched the portrait of a cowboy in Pocatello, Idaho. Drawings such as this one caught the attention of New York publishers and he was hired to illustrate western theme magazines and novels for Zane Grey, work which received favorable response.

As Johnson's career escalated, he developed a friendship with another western artist, Clyde Forsythe; and because of their mutual interests in depicting the historic west, the two artists established a studio together in California. Eventually they opened a gallery in Los Angeles, which was visited by such well respected artists as Norman Rockwell, Charlie Russell and Ed Borein. Johnson was at the height of his career as an illustrator of western life when he suddenly died of meningitis in 1939.

FRANK TENNEY JOHNSON
COWBOY, POCATELLO, IDAHO
1909
WATERCOLOR ON PAPER
7 x 5"
COLLECTION JOHN C. HOOVER

ELBRIDGE AYER BURBANK

ELBRIDGE AYER BURBANK
CHIEF JOSEPH IN COLVILLE
CIRCA 1902
PENCIL ON PAPER
13½ × 10½"
COURTESY SIDESTREET GALLERY, SANDPOINT, IDAHO

Born August 10, 1858, at Harvard, Illinois. Began art studies at the Academy of Design, Chicago, in 1874. Worked for Northwest Magazine, *used by Northern Pacific Railway to promote land sales. Traveled through Montana, Idaho, and Washington to the coast. Entered art school in Munich, Germany, in 1886 and studied four years in Europe. Returned to Chicago and specialized in painting portraits of Black children. Traveled to Western Indian reservations and painted portraits of chiefs and prominent figures, 1897-1899. Moved to Muskogee, Oklahoma, and San Francisco. Died in San Francisco, March 21, 1949.*

Just before the turn of the century, Elbridge Burbank, an Illinois painter and crayon portraitist, traveled throughout Indian territories in the West to paint Native Americans and document their lifestyles. During the course of his journeys he met and painted many renowned Indian leaders, including Red Cloud of the Sioux, Apache Chief Geronimo, and Chief Joseph of the Nez Perce.

Elbridge Burbank's upper-class family encouraged and supported his artistic endeavors. Burbank took courses of instruction in life drawing and portraiture at the Chicago Art Institute and later at the Royal Academy in Munich, Germany. On his return from Europe, he began a career in Chicago specializing in genre scenes and portraits. He first turned to the subject of American Indians in 1897 when his uncle Elbridge Ayer, the first President of the Field Columbian Museum in Chicago, commissioned Burbank to undertake a series of Native American portrait studies. This event changed his life and over the next forty years Burbank depicted representatives of more than 125 western tribes.

Burbank developed friendships with many Native Americans he encountered among various tribes. He chose portrait subjects for their character and sought to paint interesting personalities, whether they were famous or not. In his book *Burbank Among the Indians*, an account of his experiences, he writes, "The greatest Indian I have ever known was Chief Joseph, the Nez Perce—a soldier, statesman and gentleman by any standard."[1] He remarked on meeting this highly regarded chief, "He was an imposing Indian, gentle, dignified, serious. Most of my subjects sat stiff and silent while posing, but Chief Joseph conversed with me all the time I was working on his portrait."[2] Burbank and Joseph became friends; they hunted together, reminisced, and shared stories. When Chief Joseph died, Burbank reflected, "I felt that I had lost a true friend, that our country had lost a great man, and that the finest gentleman among all the real Americans had passed to his final reward."[3]

1. Burbank, E. A. *Burbank Among the Indians* (Caldwell, Idaho: Caxton Printers, 1946) 175.
2. Burbank 179.
3. Burbank 184.

MR. AND MRS. WALTER MCINTOSH

MR. & MRS. WALTER H. MCINTOSH
SOLDIER CANYON NEAR FORT LAPWAI
1886
OIL ON CANVAS
27¾ × 23¾"
COLLECTION UNIVERSITY OF IDAHO LIBRARY

Fort Lapwai was established in 1862 to prevent white encroachment on the Nez Perce Indian reservation and later served as a base to protect local settlers. First occupied by volunteer troops and subsequently garrisoned by army regulars, the Fort was active during the Nez Perce Wars of 1877.

This painting of a cavalry officer by Mr. and Mrs. Walter McIntosh depicts Soldier Canyon, a noted U.S. cavalry trail mark, near Fort Lapwai and the Nez Perce Indian mission. It was painted at Moscow, Idaho, during the winter of 1886. The McIntoshes, who lived in Moscow from 1882 to 1893, donated the painting to University of Idaho in 1940.

JAMES EVERETT STUART

Born March 24, 1852, in Maine. Moved to California with his family in 1860; settled in Sacramento. Studied with a local portrait painter, 1868-73; at California School of Design, San Francisco, 1873-78; and later in New York. Maintained studios in Ashland and Portland, Oregon, in the 1880s, and later in Chicago and New York. Moved to San Francisco in 1912 and established a studio. Died in San Francisco, January 1, 1941.

James Everett Stuart was the grandson of Gilbert Stuart, the leading portrait artist of the Federalist period, who painted America's most famous image of George Washington. Like his grandfather, James Everett Stuart was a prolific artist, producing well over five thousand paintings during his lifetime. And similar to his grandfather's art, the majority of James Stuart's work is romantic, idealized, and distinguished by quick, deft brushstrokes and surface effects.

At the age of eight James Stuart sailed with his parents from New York to San Francisco by way of the Isthmus of Panama. Early on he showed an aptitude for drawing, and after receiving art lessons in Sacramento, he attended the San Francisco School of Design and became a member of the city's Bohemian Club, the center of art activity in the city.

The first of Stuart's frequent trips to the Northwest occurred in 1876. He worked principally in Oregon, California, and Washington and at locales in Idaho, Montana, and Wyoming. By 1881 Stuart combined studio painting with intermittent trips throughout the United States and parts of Mexico and Alaska. Sparked by wanderlust, "he thoroughly covered the country, missing few lakes, mountains, and pictorial landmarks."[1] Beginning in 1900 he kept a record of his paintings by describing every scene with the exact date, place and the expected price on the reverse side of each canvas.

Considered a vain, high-living individual, Stuart maintained a studio in New York City where he produced a variety of documentary scenes, portraits, and still lifes, as well as elaborate sentimental landscapes. His studio views were normally stiff and pretentious compared to oil sketches made in the field. *Shoshone Falls*, seen from the head of the cascade instead of at the usual vantage point near the base, is executed in a freely brushed and spontaneous manner.

As an artist at the turn of the century, he was almost as well known as his grandfather, having achieved international recognition for his landscapes of the West.

1. *An Art Perspective of the Historical Northwest, from the Collection of Dr. and Mrs. Franz R. Stenzel* (Helena: Montana Historical Society, 1963) 25.

JAMES EVERETT STUART
LOOKING OVER THE TOP OF SHOSHONE FALLS, IDAHO
JUNE 1885
OIL ON CANVAS
18 × 30"
COURTESY SIDESTREET GALLERY, SANDPOINT, IDAHO

HENRY L. A. CULMER

Born in Darington, England, March 25, 1854. Immigrated to Utah with his parents in 1868. Studied with Utah artist Alfred Lambourne, California artist Julian Rix. Published writings on "Mountain Art" in Western Monthly, *1894. Paintings of Utah natural bridges published by* National Geographic *in 1907. Died February 10, 1914 at Salt Lake City. Work in Utah State Capitol Building, Utah Historical Society, B.Y.U. Art Center, University of Utah.*

Henry Culmer moved to Utah at an early age. Adept with watercolors and oils, he pursued painting from boyhood. An accountant and newspaper editor by profession, he studied art in his spare time, but remained a "weekend painter" most of his life.

An important turning point occurred when Culmer met the acclaimed artist Thomas Moran at an exhibition in Salt Lake City. The meeting profoundly affected this aspiring artist and he proceeded to develop a style similar to his mentor's. Like Moran, he painted panoramic western vistas, but his primary focus was grandiose rock-country landscapes. Interestingly, the composition for Culmer's painting *Shoshone Falls* is derived from the well-known original of the same subject by Moran.

During the last four years of his life, Culmer painted full-time, and despite few formal lessons, he gained wide recognition.

HENRY L. A. CULMER
SHOSHONE FALLS
CIRCA 1900
OIL ON CANVAS
13 × 26"
COLLECTION MUSEUM OF CHURCH HISTORY AND ART
SALT LAKE CITY

MRS. M. J. BRADLEY

MRS. M. J. BRADLEY
GEM, IDAHO AND GEM MILL
CIRCA 1890s
OIL ON CANVAS
30¾ × 45⅞"
COLLECTION CHENEY COWLES MUSEUM

Mrs. M. J. Bradley's painting *Gem, Idaho and Gem Mill* depicts a naive vision of the mining community in Idaho's panhandle region at the turn of the century. The quiet mood and simplistic presentation give no indication that during the 1890s Gem was the scene of Idaho's most famous labor dispute, where a violent conflict between union miners and the Mine Owners' Association occurred with loss of life and property.

In Bradley's interpretation, Gem appears quiet and prosperous. Although there are several people shown on the town's main street, the crisscrossing tracks, roads, and trails and the presence of two trains indicate that this a busy rural mining community. Careful attention is paid to even the smallest features and each element is thoughtfully delineated. The appeal of Bradley's painting lies in its straightforward presentation and its sensitive use of line, color, and detail. A charming overview, *Gem, Idaho and Gem Mill* offers an intimate look at an active Idaho mining town during the turn of the century.

FRANK JAY HAYNES

FRANK JAY HAYNES
UP MAIN STREET, BURKE, IDAHO
1893
CONTACT PRINT FROM ORIGINAL GLASS NEGATIVE
11 × 14"
COURTESY MONTANA HISTORICAL SOCIETY

Being in the right place at the right time afforded Frank Jay Haynes the opportunity to be retained as the official photographer for the Northern Pacific Railroad. A young and aggressive businessman from Moorhead, Minnesota, he negotiated a contract which launched a thirty-two-year career of photographing the beauty and wonders of the West. His pictures were used to promote the lands along the railway and provided visual documentation of the line's construction as it crossed the plains.

From 1876 to 1905, Haynes photographed the Northwest, taking pictures of forts, Indians, surveying parties, towns, ranches, homesteaders, miners, steamboats, and, most importantly, railroads and depot stations. In over 9,000 negatives, his photographs captured the growth and development of cities and towns along the Northern Pacific mainline and branches. Successful in his work, Haynes was assigned a railway passenger car fitted out as a studio on wheels.

In addition to being Northern Pacific Railroad's official photographer, Haynes sold his views to real estate speculators and local promoters. By 1884, Haynes' reputation was firmly established and he was given a lease by the Department of the Interior to open a studio in Yellowstone Park. For over thirty years he publicized the grandeur of the Park while continuing to document views across the Northwest.

Haynes, who took frequent trips to raw frontier towns, arrived in Burke, Idaho, a prosperous mining center, in 1893. His picture, *Up Main Street*, shows the road which was used as the primary corridor through the heart of town. The gulch in which the mining town grew up was so narrow that the hotel was constructed straddling the creek, and the railroad tracks, by necessity, ran through the center of the town. It was so cramped that "a passageway for trains went through the middle of the hotel and lodgers had to close their windows when the wood-burning locomotives steamed past."[1] The city, pinched between the mountains, was so unusual that it was once a feature for "Ripley's Believe It Or Not."

1. Conley, Cort. *Idaho for the Curious* (Cambridge, Idaho: Backeddy Books, 1981) 41

Born October 20, 1853, in Saline, Michigan. Educated in Saline public schools; apprenticed to a local photographer. Opened a studio at Moorhead, Minnesota, 1876; moved studio to Fargo, North Dakota, in 1880. Photographed throughout the Northwest as an employee of the Northern Pacific Railroad, 1876-1905. Began photographing Yellowstone in 1881; served as official park photographer, 1884-1916. Organized first stage and motorbus lines through Yellowstone; published a guide to the park in 1888. Opened a studio in St. Paul, Minnesota, in 1895. Died in St. Paul, March 10, 1921.

AUGUSTUS KOCH

The building of the transcontinental railroad spurred a thirty-year surge of settlement in Idaho. During the years 1880 to 1910, artists traveled throughout the state looking for important sites to document, thereby providing a lasting visual history of growing towns.

Augustus Koch was one of a talented corps of itinerant artists who roamed the counties of Idaho and other areas of the Northwest producing "bird's-eye" views of cities and surrounding countryside. His career began in 1868 and continued for thirty years. Illustrators such as Koch "began by moving slowly through the town and making dozens of ground level sketches of individual buildings and landscape features"[1]. They also used photographs and street maps to more accurately represent the grid pattern and layout of an area. In 1897, toward the end of his career, Augustus Koch produced this view of Moscow, Idaho, which reveals street systems and patterns of open space. Individual features like the railroad station and city center are easily recognized.

Often vignettes located at the outer edge of the print featured magnified views of important architectural structures. Here windows, roof lines, and other building details are plainly visible. Augustus Koch's 1897 lithograph is typical of hundreds of images illustrating young communities throughout the state. Artists hoped to find subscriptions for their images both from curious easterners as well as from local townspeople.

1. Reps, John W. *Panoramas of Promise*. (Pullman: Washington State University Press, 1984) 19.

Born October 15, 1840, in Birnbaum, Prussia. Immigrated to the United States at an unknown date. Served as draughtsman in the Engineer's Office of the Union army, 1861-65. Began career as a view-maker in 1868 and published his own works after 1874. Traveled to twenty-three states and produced one hundred ten known lithographs between 1868 and 1898.

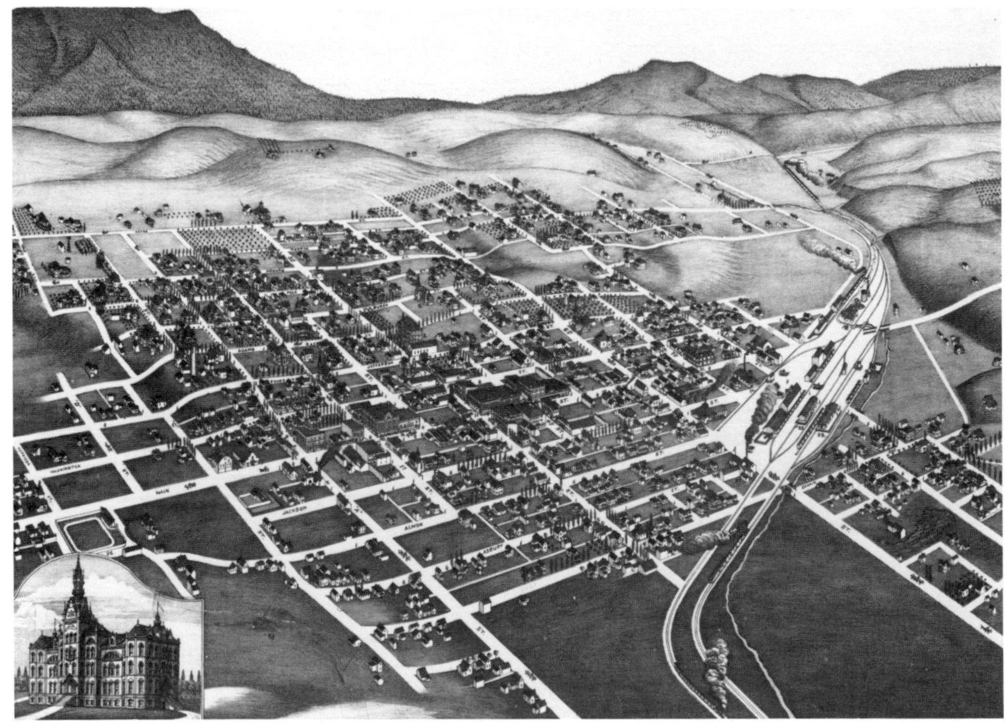

AUGUSTUS KOCH
BIRD'S EYE VIEW OF THE CITY OF MOSCOW, LATAH COUNTY, IDAHO
1897
LITHOGRAPH
24 × 32"
COLLECTION UNIVERSITY OF IDAHO LIBRARY

T. SLIGHT

T. Slight is a mystery artist. No articles or records were discovered regarding this painter's presence in Boise. However, there remains an oddly primitive but charming painting of Grove Street with its picturesque waterwheel. Grove Street was on the route of great wagon trains and dashing stage-coaches drawn by teams of horses which hauled freight and passengers to the mining camps in the Boise Basin back country. This early Boise road, which paralleled the river, was lined with green fields and wooded areas.

T. SLIGHT
GROVE STREET IN BOISE
1897
OIL ON CANVAS
29¼ × 44½"
COLLECTION IDAHO STATE HISTORICAL SOCIETY

NELLIE JANE STOCKBRIDGE

T. N. BARNARD AND NELLIE STOCKBRIDGE
PLACER MINING, DELTA
N.D.
SEPIA TONED PRINT
11 x 14"
COURTESY UNIVERSITY OF IDAHO LIBRARY

Born May 19, 1868, in Pana, Illinois. Received professional photographic training in Chicago. Moved to Wallace, Idaho, in 1898 to work as a retoucher for T. N. Barnard. Took charge of studio photography after 1898. Continued studio portraiture and advertising and promotional work after 1908 when Barnard left the business. Created a library of several thousand negatives of historical and aesthetic significance. Actively controlled the business until shortly before her death on May 22, 1965.

T. N. Barnard ventured west as a young man in 1883 at the age of twenty-two. He worked for three years learning his trade from a frontier photographer in Miles City, Montana, before moving on to the gold and silver mines of the Coeur d'Alenes. After several business ventures in Washington and Idaho, Barnard established himself in Wallace as a commercial photographer. He was a busy man, who in addition to producing portraits and promotional photography, also dabbled in mining deals, real estate, and politics. After Barnard was elected the fourth mayor of Wallace, he needed an assistant in his photography business, and in 1898 he hired Nellie Stockbridge. Their partnership of talents, his in the western tradition of photography and hers in studio portraiture, was applied to documenting Northern Idaho's citizenry, businesses, architecture, cultural activities, and important events. These photographs, which cover a period of nearly eighty years, are a visual record of the richest commercial mining district in Idaho from its earliest gold rush days until it became a settled community.

Barnard-Stockbridge photographs are best known for their representation of daily life in the Silver Valley of the Coeur d'Alenes. With what must have been great effort, the two photographers climbed surrounding mountains and trudged through formidable canyons to capture just the right views. Equipment was transported by buggy, then

THOMAS NATHAN BARNARD

T. N. BARNARD AND NELLIE STOCKBRIDGE
ROTARY SNOWPLOW ON THE S-BRIDGE
N.D.
SEPIA TONED PRINT
11 x 14"
COURTESY UNIVERSITY OF IDAHO LIBRARY

hand carried up rugged ravines to mines and mills. Assignments sometimes required hazardous descents into tunnels where pictures were made with artificial lighting. The clarity and composed placement achieved under such adverse conditions are remarkable. More than documentary photographs, these are carefully structured aesthetic images.

The railroad was North Idaho's primary link to the outside world, especially in winter. When the region was covered with heavy snowfalls, avalanches and landslides disrupted service. The photograph of the 839-foot "S" bridge, the only one of its kind at the time, was taken in the snowy canyon above Willow Creek eleven miles east of Wallace. In this image of a Northern Pacific train stranded on the trestle, one is reminded not only of the difficulty of keeping tracks clear, but of the labor required to photograph such a scene.

The images of Barnard and Stockbridge demonstrate a consistent quality, a result of technical skill and careful darkroom techniques. In her later years, Nellie Stockbridge organized and cataloged the collection of more than twenty-nine thousand negatives. After her death at the age of ninety-seven in 1965, the original dry-plate glass and flexible film negatives were donated by her heirs to the University of Idaho, where they are maintained in the University Library.

Born November 30, 1861, in Belmont County, Ohio. Grew up in Waukon, Iowa. In 1881, became apprentice to photographer Laton Huffman in Miles City, Montana. Opened his first studio in 1886 in Murray, Idaho. Moved to Wardner and then to Wallace in 1889, where his studio and many negatives were destroyed in the July 1890 fire. Photographed Northern Idaho mines, towns, and scenery; produced commissioned portraits, advertisements, periodical and book illustrations. Became involved in mining speculation, real estate, and local politics; served as mayor of Wallace 1898-1899. Hired photographer Nellie Stockbridge as his assistant in 1898. After 1908, in ill health, moved with his family to Spokane and then Los Angeles, where he died in 1916.

E. CROMBE

In Idaho, as all over the West, saloons played a central role in the drama of frontier society. A barroom was often the first public building, and as the social center of town, was one place were men could find entertainment and enjoyable works of art.

"The saloon was called the homesteader's and cowboy's art gallery."[1] On the walls one could sometimes see mountain landscapes provided by community artists, but paintings and lithographs appealing to masculine tastes were far more common. Among typical subjects were two favorites, "Custer's Last Stand" and portraits of the boxer John L. Sullivan. The most popular image, however, was that of discreetly positioned voluptuous sirens in various stages of undress. Women in these portraits rarely engage the viewer with a direct gaze, but appear detached as if in a dream. Their round and alluring forms reflected the Victorian fascination with the classical figure. Downplaying their lascivious aspect, many paintings were based on mythological themes, which lent the work an idealistic overtone.

There is no record of E. Crombe in local history, but he is most likely one of many western artists who enjoyed the sponsorship of saloon keepers and whose visions graced frontier barroom walls at the turn of the century.

1. Erdoes, Richard. *Saloons of the Old West* (New York: Knopf, 1979) 50

E. CROMBE
NUDE WOMEN
CIRCA 1890
OIL ON CANVAS
25 × 30"
COLLECTION IDAHO STATE HISTORICAL SOCIETY

MERRITT DANA HOUGHTON

Born in Otsego, Michigan, 1846. Came to Laramie, Wyoming, with his wife in 1875; also lived in Saratoga and Encampment, Wyoming. Operated an art and photography studio in Rawlins; taught in various Wyoming school districts. Wrote and published promotional booklets; illustrated C. G. Coutant's 1897 History of Wyoming. *Settled near Spokane at Hillyard, Washington, around 1907 and worked as an artist until his death during the influenza epidemic of 1919.*

Merritt Dana Houghton was a professional artist, illustrator and photographer who made his living by depicting homesteads, mining operations, logging mills, and towns in western Wyoming. For thirty years, he counted among his customers ranchers and urban businessmen who wanted pictures of their properties. In the 1890s hard times hit the lumber and mining industries of Wyoming, plummeting the local economy into a depression. Because money became tight and work unavailable, Houghton was prompted to move his art business westward to find clients in the boomtowns of Idaho and Washington.

Houghton's overview of Mullan, Idaho, was produced in 1907, when the mining camp was in full swing. Houghton's drawing, rendered from a hillside above the community, is similar to townscape panoramas popular throughout the West at the turn of the century. Compositionally, these documentary drawings usually share common characteristics: they are viewed from a high vantage point, show streets and structures laid out in detail, and describe features of individual buildings. In Houghton's bird's-eye perspective, the town looks minuscule set against the abruptly rising Coeur d'Alene Mountains.

More than any other contemporary record, this type of precise drawing allows us to visualize how Pacific Northwest frontier towns grew and changed and how they appeared to residents in their own time. Houghton's sensitive illustration, dominated by the imposing terrain, serves as a descriptive record of the remote Mullan settlement.

MERRITT DANA HOUGHTON
MULLAN, IDAHO
1907
PEN AND INK ON PAPER
17 × 26¼"
COLLECTION CHENEY COWLES MUSEUM

JOHN FERY

JOHN FERY
LAKE PEND OREILLE, IDAHO
1892
OIL ON CANVAS
45 × 80"
COLLECTION BURLINGTON RESOURCES

Born March 25, 1859 in Strasswalchen, Austria. Educated in Vienna, Dusseldorf, Karlsruhe and Munich. Visited America frequently beginning in 1886, living and painting on the East Coast for five years. Conducted tours and hunting trips for European nobility in the Rocky Mountains and the Southwest. Joined in America in the early 1890s by his wife and daughter. Employed as an artist by the Great Northern Railroad and the Oregon Journal. *Lived in Milwaukee 1903-1910 and 1923-1929, also traveling throughout the West. Moved to Orcas Island, Washington, in 1929, and to Everett, Washington, in 1930. Died September 10, 1934, and is buried on Orcas Island. Exhibited at the Columbian Exposition, Chicago, 1893. Retrospective exhibition at the Milwaukee Public Library, 1974; at the Boise Gallery of Art, 1975. Works in the collection of Burlington Northern Railroad and several private collections.*

John Fery, born of a prominent aristocratic family in Austria, received a classical education in Vienna, Dusseldorf, and Munich art academies in the 1880s. He made his first visit to the United States in 1886 and thereafter spent his time venturing to and from Austria and touring western America. Fery was so taken by the magnificent vistas of the the Rocky Mountains and Northwest that he often returned to sketch and to paint.

In 1891, on a visit to his homeland, Fery organized two extensive hunting expeditions to western states and the northern Rockies for Austrian nobility. On one of these trips Fery traveled through the panhandle of Idaho, where he sketched a study of Lake Pend Oreille. It was Fery's practice to make renderings while on tour, and later during winter months at his studio, he would transform his drawings into large-scale paintings.

Lake Pend Oreille, Idaho, an early canvas, was painted in his Munich studio in 1892. "The color is monochromatic brown and the mood has heavy overtones of romantic melancholia."[1] The dark nature of this painting was influenced by European academic styles which were popular at the turn of the century. As he spent more time in the United States, Fery's subjects became Western-oriented and his palette grew lighter in color. His canvases were primarily landscape views and wildlife scenes; rarely were there references to human figures.

In 1910 Fery was commissioned by the Great Northern Railroad to create promotional paintings for the company. He was charged with making large panoramas of landmarks along the route serviced by the railroad. From 1910 to 1930 Fery painted over three hundred monumental-sized variations on western outdoor themes, many of them majestic scenes of Glacier National Park in Montana. The paintings were displayed in stations located along the Great Northern line, as well as in hotels and commercial buildings across the nation. John Fery was a prolific artist whose enthusiasm for the natural wonders of the West is apparent in his many canvases exalting the unspoiled wilderness.

1. Walton, Ann Thorson. *The Burlington Northern Collection* (Seattle: Burlington Northern, Inc., 1982) 29.

ABBY RHODA WILLIAMS HILL

ABBY WILLIAMS HILL
CABINET GORGE, IDAHO
1904
OIL ON CANVAS
38 × 28"
COLLECTION UNIVERSITY OF PUGET SOUND

Abby Williams Hill was well trained as an artist, having studied in Chicago and New York. After her marriage to Dr. Frank Hill, she and her husband moved from the Midwest to Tacoma, Washington, in 1889. Enamored of the grandeur of the northern landscape, Abby Hill began to paint outdoor views in the "hope of arousing interest in the preservation of our scenery."[1]

In the summer of 1904, Abby Williams Hill agreed to paint for the Northern Pacific Railroad Company in exchange for a railroad pass. Promising to provide the company with ten canvases, Abby Hill set out with her four children, tents, and painting equipment to document the railway route through the North Cascades and Rocky Mountains in Idaho and Montana.

Toward the end of summer, Abby and her brood camped in the Coeur d'Alene range. The air, usually crystal clear, was plagued by the smoke of forest fires which ran rampant in Idaho and Washington in 1904. She complained that the haze obstructed the views which in turn affected the painting process. In a rush to escape an intense blaze near Hope, Idaho, she and her children scrambled aboard a train bound to Cabinet Gorge, up the Clark Fork Valley.

Cabinet Gorge is one of her canvases from this journey depicting an Idaho location. In this painting, the cliff pinnacles create strong geometric shapes. In Abby Hill's journal she notes this poetic comment: "The Gorge is a beautiful sight, iron stained slate, which of itself is very veined. The color, sometimes masses of lavender, then again, green prevails. At times, the rock looks like mat, at others, it is rough and seamed. The river is very placid at this season and a beautiful green, deep or light as it flows in shadow or sunlight and just glinted with the colors of the rocks which tower above it."[2] In this painting, typical of her Northwest work, the artist achieves a powerful sense of space with soft pastel colors and bold forms.

1. Appleton, M. B. *Who's Who in Northwest Art* (Seattle: McCaffrey, 1941) 34.
2. Fields, Ronald. *Abby Williams Hill and the Lure of the West* (Tacoma: Washington State Historical Society, 1988) 56.

Born September 25, 1861 in Grinnell, Iowa. Studied at Art Institute of Chicago 1882-84; Art Students League, with William Merritt Chase, 1888; in Munich with Herman Haase, 1896; at Corcoran Gallery, 1904. Painted twenty-one canvases in North Cascades for Great Northern Railway, 1903. Painted for Northern Pacific Railway in Northwest and Yellowstone, 1904-06; visited Flathead and Nez Perce reservations to paint portraits. Traveled widely throughout West and Europe with her children. Moved to California in 1910 because of her husband's illness. Lived at Laguna Beach, 1913-21; camped and painted in national parks, 1924-31. Died in San Diego, California, in 1943. Paintings displayed at Louisiana Purchase Exposition, St. Louis (1904); Lewis and Clark Exposition, Portland (1905); Jamestown Tricentennial (1907); Alaska-Yukon-Pacific Exposition, Seattle (1909). Over one hundred of her works are in the collection of the University of Puget Sound.

MARY HALLOCK FOOTE

Artist and author Mary Hallock Foote arrived in the small western outpost of Boise in 1884. Her background was Eastern; she was a cultivated woman educated in New York, who by circumstance of marriage was transplanted to the West. Conveying a sensitivity to the conditions of frontier life, she expressed anguish at being exiled from sophisticated urban society to the barren cultural soil of the West. An illustrator, painter, engraver, and author, she chronicled her Western experiences in stories for East Coast magazines.

Married to the enterprising civil engineer Arthur DeWint Foote, she accompanied her husband to project sites throughout the West during the late nineteenth century. Beginning in 1877, she wrote and illustrated articles for *Scribner's Monthly* on life in California mining camps. With the popularity of these pieces, she attained a New York following and a reputation as a writer and illustrator of Western fiction. After travels to California, Colorado, and Mexico she came to Idaho in 1884 for a ten-year sojourn.

Mary Hallock Foote's numerous publications include twelve novels plus a variety of articles and short stories on Western life. Her most successful works were inspired in Idaho. A full-length novel entitled *The Chosen Valley* and several fictional stories deal with the struggle to bring water to the farms of Boise, at that time an isolated territorial capital and county seat adjacent to a small army post.

During his years in Boise, Arthur Foote's engineering project was the design of an irrigation system based on damming and diverting the Boise River. Reminiscent of the

Born November 19, 1847, in Milton, New York. Moved to New York City in 1864 to attend the School of Design, Cooper Union, in order to become a professional illustrator; later studied with genre painter Frost Johnson and wood engraver W. J. Linton. Came to the West in 1876 following her marriage to Arthur DeWint Foote. Wrote and illustrated a dozen published novels and numerous stories and articles for Scribner's Monthly, The Century, *and* St. Nicholas Magazine *while living in New Almaden and Santa Cruz, California; Leadville, Colorado; Mexico; Boise, Idaho (1884-93); and Grass Valley, California. Died in Boston, Massachusetts, June 25, 1938.*

MARY HALLOCK FOOTE
A PRETTY GIRL IN THE WEST
CENTURY MAGAZINE, OCTOBER 1889
PENCIL AND WASH ON PAPER
5½ × 7⅞"
COLLECTION LIBRARY OF CONGRESS, WASHINGTON, D.C.

canals still in use today is the image *Between the Desert and the Sown* from "The Conquest of Arid America," published by *Century Magazine* in 1895. This windswept barren landscape cut through by an artery of water foreshadows the future of large-scale irrigation in southern Idaho. Irrigation canals such as those pictured by Mary Hallock Foote made possible the settlement and cultivation of the sagebrush plains.

For *Century Magazine* in 1888-89, she wrote and illustrated an Idaho series, "Pictures of the Far West," which remains one of her most successful works. These illustrated stories are autobiographical in that they are based upon settings and episodes which she personally observed. The scene from "A Pretty Girl in the West" is an example of Mary Hallock Foote's transformation of her surroundings, the veranda of her own stone house in Boise River Canyon, to an illustration for a fictional story. Although her images and dialogue tend to be romanticized, as was the popular style of the day, Mary Hallock Foote sought to express an attitude in which "the West is not to be measured by homesick tales from an Eastern point of view."[1]

Working from the middle 1870s to the First World War, she accomplished a written and visual document of the West's "social genesis." One of Idaho's most interesting literary and artistic figures, Mary Hallock Foote became the subject of Wallace Stegner's Pulitzer Prize novel *Angle of Repose*, published in 1971, which is based on her career.

1. Maguire, James H. *Mary Hallock Foote* (Boise: Boise State College, 1972) 44.

MARY HALLOCK FOOTE
BETWEEN THE DESERT AND THE SOWN
CENTURY MAGAZINE, MAY 1895
PENCIL AND WASH ON PAPER
6⅞ × 10"
COLLECTION LIBRARY OF CONGRESS, WASHINGTON, D.C.

BUILDING A STATE

JULIAN E. ITTER
MINERS AND CABIN
CIRCA 1900
OIL ON CANVAS
11½ × 16¼"
COLLECTION CHENEY COWLES MUSEUM

The territorial boundaries of Idaho encompassed a wide variety of geographic features. Below the Snake River, along the northern edge of the Great Basin, the land is arid; the central mountains are jagged and forbidding, while to the north lies the gentler rolling timberland of the panhandle. Idaho's early residents were as diverse as the topography of the state. The Southeast was settled by Mormon missionaries and homesteaders, while the mining and lumber industries attracted rugged individualists to the northern panhandle and central mountain region. The remoteness of the state also attracted a contingent of Civil War veterans, both Yankee and Confederate soldiers, who had broken with the past to start over in Idaho mining camps. This dichotomy of land and people seemed an unlikely combination for a unified state, especially when northern miners associated themselves with business and culture in Spokane, while in the south, agricultural communities maintained an alliance with Salt Lake City. And yet Idaho, in spite of its physical barriers and lack of social and political unity, became a state in 1890.

The population of Idaho has from its earliest days been sparse. When settlements and towns began to develop, they were located at opposite ends of the state, restricting the easy exchange of ideas; travel between north and south remained arduous and was not extensive. Artists who settled in Idaho towns received little outside visual or cultural stimulation, and although some individuals had studied in prestigious art centers in the eastern United States and Europe, their works often acquired a naive quality after extended periods of living in cultural isolation. In addition, financial incentives for artists were lacking. Idaho did not have affluent art collectors nor were its wealthy mining magnates in residence; thus patronage was minimal and locally confined.

For rural residents and small town citizens there was little available in the way of real art experiences. Idaho's first organized art exhibitions occurred in the 1870s. In Boise City, amateur artists participated in local exhibits, often fundraisers, such as the one hosted in a Grove Street mansion to benefit a "Free Reading Room," or an 1872 show held for the Baptist church which drew fifty-two entries. Toward the 1880s, several art displays were installed at the fairgrounds offering cash prizes to the winners. By granting awards in categories such as "best fruit painting" or "best flower painting," these fairs encouraged the representation of particular scenes and subjects. When shows occurred, nearly all entrants were women and many of the artists' submissions were copies of well-known pictures.

From its commencement, The Idaho Intermountain Fair generated an audience for local exhibitors and was a catalyst for bringing artists together. On October 17, 1898, The Statesman reported, "Last night a large group of art enthusiasts met in the art department of the exposition building to form a state art association. Officers were elected from Lewiston, Boise, and Pocatello. The Intermountain Fair attracted the state's best artists with J. P. McMeekin winning most of the prizes."[1] Early fairs and expositions provided a forum where artists were able to display their works, but from a professional standpoint, Idaho had no real art communities or societies like those found in Washington, Colorado, or Utah.

After the turn of the century, because few Idaho exhibiting opportunities were available, many amateur and professional artists turned to regional and national expositions to exhibit their artwork. The Lewis and Clark Exposition in Portland; the Alaska-Yukon-Pacific Exposition in Seattle; and the Panama-Pacific International Exposition in San Francisco, as well as art associations in Washington and Utah, offered arenas in which Idaho artists could present their creative efforts.

1. Hart, Arthur. "Grove Street Mansion Housed 1892 Art Exhibit." *Idaho Statesman* 14 August 1989: 3D.

EMMA EDWARDS GREEN

EMMA EDWARDS GREEN
STATE SEAL OF IDAHO
1892
OIL ON CANVAS
30 × 30"
COLLECTION IDAHO STATE HISTORICAL SOCIETY

Born 1858 in Stockton, California, daughter of John C. Edwards, governor of Missouri and later mayor of Stockton. Studied art for one year in New York City before moving to Boise in 1890. Taught school in Horseshoe Bend, Bruneau, Atlanta, and the Seven Devils country, and taught summer art classes in her Boise studio. Married to mining engineer James G. Green. Moved to California, where her husband died in 1933. Lived in Oakland, then returned to Boise shortly before her death. Died January 6, 1942, in Boise, and is buried in Oakland, California.

Emma Edwards Green arrived in Boise to visit cousins in 1890 shortly after Idaho achieved statehood. She was the oldest of eight children, had attended art school in New York, and was considered a well-educated woman of her time. The daughter of a Missouri governor, Emma took more than a passing interest in Idaho politics. She was an attractive young woman with an affable personality and was readily accepted into Boise society, where she met many local politicians.

An initial action of the new state legislature was to order the creation of a state seal. A competition was organized, and because of her artistic talents and statehouse friendships, Emma was invited to participate. She interviewed politicians, listened to their suggestions, and proceeded to select insignia for a dignified state emblem. Her remarks are of interest: "I must embody the resources, principally mining, so I put a miner on the seal; woman's suffrage was coming so I put a woman on the seal opposite him to signify the equality between the sexes."[1] To represent the resources and characteristics of Idaho, she chose wild syringa, the state flower; a sheaf of grain for agriculture; a towering pine for abundant timber; and a miner's pick for the mineral industry. The design was submitted and immediately accepted as the official state seal.

Emma Green taught art in Boise for several years before marrying James Green, who was prominent in the mining business. She accompanied him on his explorations in Idaho, often painting vistas along the way. When not traveling in the mountains she spent time at their home on Grove Street in Boise. An ambitious and energetic person, she worked for the cause of woman suffrage and edited the society page of the *Evening Capital News*. Emma continued to paint Idaho landscapes and mining scenes for over fifty years. Purported to be the only woman to design a state seal, Emma Green made a lasting contribution to art in Idaho.

1. Dawdy, Doris O. *Artists of the American West* (Chicago: Sage Books, 1974-85) Vol. 2: 111.

HERBERT A. COLLINS

HERBERT A. COLLINS
FRANK STEUNENBERG
1911-12
OIL ON CANVAS
29½ × 24½"
COLLECTION IDAHO STATE HISTORICAL SOCIETY

In the winter of 1911, James H. Hawley, then acting governor of Idaho, was looking for a competent artist to paint the portraits of past territorial and state governors. Quite by accident, attorney Jess Hawley, the governor's son, discovered that one of his clients, Herbert Collins from Hagerman, was once a thriving artist in the Midwest. Collins submitted a proposal, and soon thereafter, he was commissioned to paint twenty portraits, including incumbent Governor Hawley and all former governors of Idaho.

Collins had been a successful portraitist in Chicago, where he maintained a studio for nineteen years. He had previously painted high-ranking public officials, counting among his clients generals, governors, senators, and even the president of Mexico. Collins received his training in Canada under a miniaturist and later studied for a year in London, where he was especially attracted by the rich dark portraits painted by Rembrandt that he saw in the National Gallery.

For health reasons, Collins was encouraged by his doctors to leave the Chicago area and move to a drier climate. He traded his home in the city for an eighty-acre tract of land near Bliss, Idaho, and headed west to become a gentleman farmer. Life was more rugged than imagined; water was scarce and it was difficult to clear the acres of sagebrush. A tenacious individual, Collins overcame these obstacles and was soon coaxing crops of wheat and alfalfa from the harsh land. For ten years, Collins interspersed farming with painting, executing portraits and a number of landscapes.

His portrait of Frank Steunenberg depicts "the governor who never wore a tie" on the grounds that it was "useless adornment." Steunenberg held office during a clamorous period in the state's history. During the combative labor disputes in the Coeur d'Alene Mining District, he declared martial law and called in federal troops against the wishes of union labor. As a direct result of his intervention, six years later Steunenberg was assassinated, blown up by dynamite as he entered the side gate of his Caldwell, Idaho, home. The story of the labor conflicts and Steunenberg's subsequent death is one of the most notorious in Idaho history.

Born in 1865 in Ontario, Canada. Apprenticed to Toronto portraitist J. W. Forster and briefly managed his studio. Moved to Omaha in 1884, painted portraits of prominent citizens; married Mary Straight in 1888. Moved to Chicago in 1890 and maintained his studio there for 19 years. Became a U.S. citizen in 1893. Due to ill health, moved in 1909 to Idaho and developed a farm four miles from Hagerman. Moved to Gooding in 1919; employed as professor of art at Gooding College. Moved to Berkeley, California, and worked for Western Museum Laboratories, National Park Service, 1934-37. Produced dioramas, historical landscapes, portraits of John Muir and Congressman William Kent, donor of Muir Woods, and of Park Service Directors. Died in 1937.

TOURTELLOTTE AND HUMMEL

Tourtellotte and Hummel building projects appear like stepping stones across the state and comprise a fifty year architectural history. The breadth and consistency of their structural designs survive in edifices throughout the intermountain region. Significantly, their commissions defined the appearance of the capital city. The majority of Boise landmarks—the Capitol Building, St. John's Cathedral, the Egyptian Theatre, the Carnegie Library, and the Hotel Boise, as well as numerous downtown commercial buildings and historic homes—were designed by Tourtellotte and Hummel.

John Everett Tourtellotte came to Boise in 1890 at the age of twenty-three. He is described as an affable, handsome, confident, self-made architect. With a knack for promotion, Tourtellotte established what was soon a flourishing business. The second principal of the firm, Charles Hummel, a native of Germany, joined the company in 1900. He immigrated to the United States and worked as a builder and architect for fifteen years before entering partnership with Tourtellotte. Educated in Germany, with years of experience as a civil engineer in Switzerland, he brought considerable expertise to the venture. Biographical sources indicate that Tourtellotte's energies were devoted primarily to business promotion while Hummel was responsible for many of the chief designs and the greater share of key works between 1900 and 1920.

TOURTELLOTTE AND COMPANY,
ARCHITECTS
IDAHO STATE CAPITOL
PRESENTATION DRAWING
1909
GRAPHITE, INK, AND WATERCOLOR ON BOARD
$51\frac{1}{2} \times 38\frac{3}{4}$
COURTESY HUMMEL, LAMARCHE & HUNSUCKER
ARCHITECTS, P.A.

The plum architectural commission in Idaho during the early 1900s was the design for the new state capitol building. With careful planning and forethought, city fathers selected a site in a prime central location at the head of what was to become Capitol Boulevard, the city's gateway. The legislature preferred to hire local architects, and Tourtellotte and Hummel rose to the challenge. Their design was a formal classic building reminiscent of the nation's Capitol: "Like contemporaries in Arkansas, Mississippi, Minnesota and Kentucky, the Idaho capitol adheres with great strictness to the model set by the Capitol in Washington, D.C., wherein a unifying dome between balanced wings expresses a bicameral legislative system, and archaeologically correct classical ornament expresses the American notion of Roman republican virtues."[1] Set against the background of the Boise foothills, this grand scale structure, built of local sandstone quarried from the Table Rock formation, became the city's most commanding landmark.

The firm's influence continues today through the efforts of several generations of Hummel family architects and their associates. Over the years, consistent quality of design, adapted to tastes of individual clients and changing times, has assured their success and continues to model the architectural character of Idaho.

1. Wright, Patricia, and Lisa B. Reitzes. *Tourtellotte and Hummel of Idaho: The Standard Practice of Architecture* (Logan: Utah State University Press, 1987) 44.

TOURTELLOTTE AND COMPANY,
ARCHITECTS
UNIVERSITY OF IDAHO
ADMINISTRATION BUILDING
PRESENTATION DRAWING BY M. HALLOWELL
1908
INK ON PAPER
22 × 30"
COURTESY HUMMEL, LAMARCHE & HUNSUCKER
ARCHITECTS, P.A.

KIRTLAND KELSEY CUTTER

KIRTLAND KELSEY CUTTER
IDAHO STATE BUILDING FOR THE WORLD'S COLUMBIAN EXPOSITION
1892
INK WASH ON PAPER
19¾ × 31¼"
COLLECTION LARRY SCHOONOVER

Born in Cleveland, Ohio, in 1860. Attended Brooks Military Academy; studied at Art Students League in New York and also in Europe. Moved to Spokane Falls, Washington, in 1885. Operated an architectural firm from before 1889 to 1923, first in partnership with John Poetz and later with Karl Gunnar Malmgren; after 1917 Cutter worked alone. As leading architect in the area, designed residences and apartments, businesses, warehouses, schools, and various other structures. Moved to Long Beach, California, in 1923 and continued residential design. Died in Long Beach in 1939.

When the newly established State of Idaho wanted representation at the World's Columbian Exposition of 1893 held in Chicago, the prominent Spokane architectural firm of K. K. Cutter was unanimously selected to design a building which would reflect a strong regional image and state identity.

K. K. Cutter's reputation was firmly established in Spokane, which was the cultural hub of prosperous northern Idaho and eastern Washington. Cutter's formal education took place in New York and included several years at the Art Students League. Like many students of the Victorian era, he toured Europe to broaden his education after graduation. He came west at the urging of his uncle, a Spokane banker, to form an architectural partnership. After a devastating fire destroyed most of downtown Spokane in 1889, Cutter's services were greatly in demand. As a result his business flourished and his ability as a talented architect was recognized. Among his many projects were commercial structures and prestigious homes for the wealthy.

To design the Exposition building, Cutter drew upon his European travel experiences. It must have occurred to Cutter that the high mountain chalets of Austria and Switzerland were perfectly suited to the rugged and remote mountains of Idaho. He incorporated expansive overhangs typical of chalets and included sparsely placed roof boulders as elements of the design. The timber and stone structure was also a glamorous reinterpretation of pioneer log cabins on a mammoth scale. In the minds of most Easterners, Idaho still remained an unknown land somewhere at the far corner of the continent. The exotic nature of the structure helped perpetuate the myth of an exotic and foreign place.

The lodge was erected in Chicago, but at the end of the fair, the Idaho building was sold at auction to a local resident and moved to Wisconsin. The log cabin was used as a summer home, but was finally neglected and fell into disrepair. It remained vacant and gained a reputation for being haunted by Idaho cowboys.

W. THOMAS SMITH

W. THOMAS SMITH
MRS. CHARLOTTE FINCH, HAYDEN LAKE
1906
OIL ON CANVAS
38 × 27½"
COLLECTION CHENEY COWLES MUSEUM

W. Thomas Smith was an English artist who settled in Spokane around 1903 and became influential in local art circles. His clientele included the social elite of Spokane and of Idaho's northern panhandle. One such patron was entrepreneur John A. Finch, a wealthy magnate who had made his fortune developing the mining industry of the Coeur d'Alene district.

In 1896, Finch married the impetuous, beautiful young Charlotte Swingler, daughter of a poor pioneer family that had come to Spokane from Minnesota in 1884. After their marriage, Finch engaged the services of Spokane's leading architect, his friend K. K. Cutter, to plan an eighteen-room mansion with an art gallery for the couple. Upon its completion Cutter was commissioned to design a palatial summer home with surrounding gardens at Hayden Lake, Idaho.

Finch, originally from England, was a philanthropist and patron of the arts with a taste for literature, horticulture, and fine painting. When this prominent businessman wished to commission a portrait of his wife, he turned to English artist W. Thomas Smith, a resident of Spokane who painted in the British romantic tradition and had exhibited work at the Royal Academy in London. The portrait of Charlotte Finch was painted in 1906 at Hayden Lake, probably in the summer when the flowers were in full bloom. The portrait is rendered in a soft lyrical style reminiscent of English portrait paintings of the nineteenth century. Smith uses flowing brush strokes, favors pastel colors, and minimizes the formality of the composition.

When Finch died unexpectedly at his Hayden Lake home in 1915, he left the greater portion of his three million dollar estate to his wife Charlotte. Mrs. Finch remarried a retired captain of a shipping fleet and moved away to California, where she died in 1945.

Resident of London, England, 1895-1901; resident of Spokane, Washington, 1903-1910. President of Spokane Society of Washington Artists, 1908. Exhibited in Spokane with Art League, 1908; Spokane Society, 1909.

JOSEPH PATRICK MCMEEKIN

The paintings of Joseph McMeekin offer a "time capsule" view of rural southern Idaho between 1890 and 1910. For over twenty years he lived at Millet Island and painted the atmospheric landscape of the Snake River Canyon near Hagerman.

Originally from Ireland, McMeekin settled with his sister's family on a homestead in a secluded section of the Snake River where basalt cliffs line the horizon. With no formal training, but with great passion for portraying nature, he recorded agrarian life. Genre scenes representing daily events are depicted in an impressionist style. Farmers clearing sagebrush, livestock huddled against winter gales, hay barges at the river's edge, and spring plowing all reflect pioneer life beneath the canyon walls. Among his most impressive landscapes are images of Snake River Canyon and Shoshone Falls. Described in velvety purples, the rock cliffs glow with a subtle blue haze which descends on the volcanic formations.

A plein air painter fascinated by the transience of nature, McMeekin depicted all hours of day in every season: "He braved snow storms, rain, and summer heat to get his

Born April 6, 1857, in Dublin, Ireland. Studied art in Ireland before immigrating to Utah with his family in 1872. Became a U.S. citizen in 1880. Moved to Millet Island in the Snake River near Hagerman in the late 1880s. Moved in 1910 to Napa, California; maintained a studio at Coombsville and made painting excursions in northern California. Worked within Napa County after 1916. Died on February 12, 1936. Exhibited at World's Columbian Exposition, Chicago, 1893; Idaho Fair, Boise, 1896; Idaho Intermountain Fair, Boise, 1902; Lewis and Clark Exposition, Portland, 1905; with the San Francisco Art Association 1911-1916; and in Napa County exhibitions.

JOSEPH P. MCMEEKIN
GEMS OF THE DESERT
1909
OIL ON CANVAS
24 x 36"
COLLECTION IDAHO STATE HISTORICAL SOCIETY

images as directly from nature as he could."[1] Winter tempests did not deter his ambition, but his obsession with art did cause him hardship—he frequently went without eating and suffered ill health from relentless painting excursions.

Living privately and in relative obscurity, McMeekin was devoted to his vocation and did not pursue marriage or family. In 1904, he opened a small gallery in Hagerman, which featured stereopticon views of southern Idaho in addition to a selection of his own oil, tempera, and gouache paintings, but the undertaking was never financially successful. McMeekin moved to California in 1910, where he responded to the scenery of his new surroundings, but he never altogether abandoned the images of the Snake River Canyon inspired by his memories.

1. *Island in the Snake: The Idaho Paintings of Pioneer Artist J. P. McMeekin* (Boise: Idaho Historical Museum, 1983) 2.

JOSEPH P. MCMEEKIN
BRUSH GATHERERS ON MILLET ISLAND
1910
OIL ON CANVAS
13¾ × 23¾"
COLLECTION IDAHO STATE HISTORICAL SOCIETY

FRANK PALMER

FRANK PALMER
THE NARROWS AT TWIN LAKES, IDAHO
CIRCA 1912
SEPIA TONED PRINT
10½ × 13½"
COURTESY EASTERN WASHINGTON STATE HISTORICAL SOCIETY

Came to Washington State from Atchison, Kansas; arrived in Spokane in 1898. Established his photography business around 1907. Until his death in 1920, worked in collaboration with his wife, Frances, who then continued to make prints for another ten years. Palmer photographic negative collection now owned by Eastern Washington State Historical Society, Spokane.

Early photographers often went to great lengths to capture exceptional scenes. One such dedicated photographer was Frank Palmer, a Spokane resident, who made frequent trips through northern Idaho and eastern Washington during the early years of the twentieth century. According to his journals, in 1908 he logged more than 4,000 miles photographing the regional countryside. Traveling by any means available — steamboat, rowboat, launch, stage, and pack horse — he made his way to the remote environs of north Idaho's farming, lake, and mountain districts.

Palmer was a commercial photographer whose images were often used for promotion. His clients included railroads, steamship lines and numerous business enterprises. Companies such as the Great Northern and Northern Pacific railways used Palmer's photographic images to illustrate brochures extolling the scenic beauty and wonders of the area. Palmer also took advantage of a thriving postcard market, an industry which flourished as a result of Pacific Northwest expansion between 1904 and 1914. He is reported to have sold 15,000 photographic cards to fulfill public demand during 1910 alone.

Frank Palmer is recognized not only for the quality of his photographs, but for the extensive inventory of work he produced on a wide variety of subjects. His aggressive picture-taking efforts provide a visual record of a rapidly changing era. Palmer sought merely to make a living as a commercial photographer, but through his success he left a rich documentary heritage.

FEODOR VON LUERZER

FEODOR VON LUERZER
FOREST FIRE IN NORTH IDAHO WOODS
1910
OIL ON BURLAP
28 × 41"
COLLECTION JACK SPURGEON

Feodor von Luerzer was a dashing man of culture descended from German nobility. Brought up in Salzburg, Austria, he was widely read, well educated, a musician, actor, artisan, painter and a man with an adventurous spirit. In 1886 the artist was recruited by the American Panorama Company of Milwaukee, Wisconsin, to assist in painting a cyclorama, one of the huge panoramic paintings of historical events and spectacular views that were a fashionable form of entertainment in the late nineteenth century.

Three years after his arrival in Wisconsin, von Luerzer embarked on an extended canoe trip from the Canadian shoreline of the Great Lakes. Arriving in Duluth, Minnesota, he established a painting studio and married a young woman from a local family. Von Luerzer's spirit of adventure once again prompted him to journey through new territory. The couple explored the Dakotas on horseback and traveled by train through Montana, Idaho, Washington, Oregon, and California.

In 1908 on a trip to explore the waterways of Washington and Idaho, the von Luerzers visited Coeur d'Alene. The broad blue lake set against picturesque mountains reminded the artist of his homeland. Charmed by the extraordinary scenery, the von Luerzers left their Duluth home to build a rustic pine cottage decorated with interior murals. The artist was quoted: "I always spend my summers here, at the Lucerne of America, as I have named Lake Coeur d'Alene. I was born in Salzburg and traveled all over Europe before coming to America, and I have found nothing more beautiful than this lake, nothing more inspiring for an artist, not even Switzerland."[1]

Miss L. Byrd Mock, a magazine writer and regular summer visitor to the lake, met von Luerzer and commissioned him to paint a series of canvases of the St. Joe River and the Coeur d'Alene hills. The twelve studies, now known as the Byrd Mock Murals, totaled sixty feet in length, showing scenes of the lake and surrounding countryside. One panel describes the cataclysmic Idaho fire of 1910 in which flames, raging from the Salmon River country to the Canadian border, destroyed three million acres and devastated the forests of north Idaho and Montana. The event had such a profound effect on von Luerzer that he included it with his characteristic views of the area.

1. Mock, L. Byrd. "The Lucerne of America." *Overland Monthly* January 1911.

Born February 14, 1851, in the province of Salzburg, Austria. Educated by tutors, in private military academies, and imperial officers' school. Studied at the Vienna Academy of Art; learned to paint murals in Munich. Came to the United States in 1886; lived in Cleveland and Milwaukee before opening a studio in Duluth, 1889. Taught, painted landscapes, decorations of Brautigam Gardens amusement park, murals in Pickwick Tavern. Married Ella Brautigam, 1897, and began extensive western travels. Became U.S. citizen, 1904. Spent a year painting in California. In 1909, moved to Coeur d'Alene, Idaho, where his brothers-in-law owned a boatworks; maintained winter residence and studio in Spokane. Died August 19, 1913, in Spokane.

IDELLA ROGERS CHESTER

IDELLA ROGERS CHESTER
BOISE RIVER BELOW ATLANTA
CIRCA 1909
OIL ON CANVAS
19¾ x 15¾"
COLLECTION MR. AND MRS. JOSEPH A. CHESTER

Idella Rogers was born in Sherbrook, Quebec, Canada in 1865. After her marriage ended, moved to Boston with her daughter, Ruperta, and then to her brother's farm at Selma, California. Came to Boise in 1895 to marry Horace Chester, a miner and building contractor. Lived in Atlanta until the town burned around 1910; taught school briefly at Soldier, near Fairfield. Lived in the North End of Boise until moving to Oregon around 1919. Died in 1943.

A strong-minded woman, Idella Rogers left Quebec, Canada, in 1892 after a divorce and traveled to the United States with her young daughter, Ruperta. She went first to Boston to visit relatives and then journeyed overland to California. Living near Fresno with her brother, a farmer, Idella commuted to San Francisco where she attended art classes.

In California, she re-connected with her childhood sweetheart Horace Chester, a miner who was then living in Atlanta, Idaho. He invited Idella and her ten-year-old daughter to come to Boise, where the couple was married on Valentine's Day, 1895, at the Overland Hotel. Before mother and daughter set out through the mountains to make their home in the Atlanta mining camp, Idella purchased art supplies from a local store.

Although she painted numerous landscapes similar to *Boise River Above Atlanta*, Idella was primarily an easel painter who enjoyed working at home and selling paintings to local residents. On one occasion, Idella painted a canvas of a semi-nude woman. The finished piece was sold to wealthy miner. When she discovered it was hung in the town saloon, she marched right down to the bar and demanded it back. On another occasion this feisty woman interrupted a gathering of locals who were imbibing in the roadway.

RUPERTA CHESTER
GREENBACK STAMP MILL, ATLANTA
CIRCA 19[illegible]
OIL ON CANVAS
22¾ × 14½"
COLLECTION MR. AND MRS. JOSEPH A. CHESTER

When offered a drink, she took the jug over her shoulder and walked back to her house, with the jug turned upside down and liquor dripping to the ground. On this issue, she wasn't challenged. An outspoken suffragette, she was an energetic advocate of woman's rights.

Ruperta, Idella's daughter, was a friendly, outgoing girl who wrote poetry. She attended Central School in Boise and in 1901, at age seventeen, married Albert Chester, her stepfather's younger brother. They resided in a house on 13th Street in Boise and spent summers in Atlanta. Ruperta often packed her art supplies and headed into the mountains to paint. As mining was the only industry in Atlanta, the mills, miners' cabins, and features of the surrounding town were a natural choice for subject matter. In *Greenback Mill* she depicts a stamp mill which had been shipped piece by piece from Chico, California, and assembled near the town to process high-grade ore.

In early Boise City and in remote Atlanta, dominated by prospectors and miners, Idella Rogers and Ruperta Chester were a bright spot of refinement and artistic intensity. After more than twenty-five years living in southwest Idaho, the mother and daughter departed. Idella Rogers set off for Portland and Ruperta Chester moved to a cattle ranch in Baker County, Oregon.

Ruperta Chester was born in Quebec in 1884; moved with her mother to Boise in 1895. Graduated from Boise schools. In 1901, married Albert Chester, a miner and teamster. Exhibited paintings at Boise area fairs. Moved to Oregon following the death of her husband in 1920. Died in Oregon, 1954.

ROBERT W. LIMBERT

ROBERT W. LIMBERT
ELK
CIRCA 1915
OIL ON CANVAS
32 × 40"
COLLECTION IDAHO STATE HISTORICAL SOCIETY

Born April 24, 1885, in southern Minnesota; grew up and received his education in Omaha, Nebraska. Learned the taxidermy business in Omaha and worked in Minnesota and Colorado before moving to Boise in 1911; opened his own business in 1913. Died in Cheyenne, Wyoming, while returning to Boise from travels, June 15, 1933.

On viewing Robert Limbert's wildlife painting of an elk in the Idaho wilderness, one might rightly guess that Limbert was a man devoted to the study of animal life and natural history. Limbert, who was originally from Omaha, Nebraska, took up the study and business of taxidermy as a young man. He came to Boise in 1911 at the age of twenty-nine and because of his skills and previous experience in tanning and mounting, he was hired as manager for a furrier and taxidermy establishment. His talent earned him a considerable reputation, and, having achieved local acclaim, he was asked to prepare the Idaho exhibition for the Panama-Pacific International Exposition in 1915. He spent several years painting reproductions of Idaho scenic wonders and gathering and preparing specimens, as well as working fourteen months in San Francisco organizing the exhibition layout. The project, designed and installed by Limbert, received prestigious awards including two medals of honor. A contemporary account states, "The exhibit was artistic as well as educational and it was the attention paid to the small details that enabled Idaho to win the Medal of Honor on arrangement and decoration."[1]

Limbert was widely recognized throughout the Northwest in his professional capacity and as an author and lecturer on natural history. This prominent Idaho naturalist, who was fond of outdoor sports, especially hunting and fishing, was acknowledged as a local artist of animal subjects and ranked as one of the best taxidermists in Idaho.

1. Hawley, James H. *History of Idaho, The Gem of the Mountains* (Chicago: S. J. Clarke, 1920) 653.

GILBERT
BOISE-ROCHESTER MILL, ATLANTA
1916-17
OIL ON CANVAS
24½ × 29¼"
COLLECTION IDAHO STATE HISTORICAL SOCIETY

During the nineteenth century, it was a common practice for East Coast artists to make their way by painting portraits and picturing farms, residences, and local businesses. Artists went from door to door soliciting commissions to earn their keep. In the West, such artisans depicted settlers and their homes, ranches, and new commercial establishments in exchange for food, lodging, and payment.

Gilbert's picture of the *Boise-Rochester Mill, Atlanta* was painted between 1915 and 1917 for room and board. He stayed at a private household in the mining town of Atlanta during its heyday and used his talents to secure his livelihood.

MARIE IRVIN

A demure Victorian woman, Marie Irvin came overland by train from New York and was immediately captivated by the frontier atmosphere and beauty of the rising Boise foothills. She arrived in Boise in 1898, a period in Idaho's history on the cusp between the old and the new, between pioneer days and the state in its dawn of development. Charmed by what she saw, Marie Irvin stayed on in the city to share her talents with local residents as a fine-arts instructor.

Marie Irvin's art training reads like a "who's who" in reputable art schools of the day. She attended Cooper Union in New York, the Boston Museum School of Art, and Columbia University and studied under well-known artist William Metcalf. With her impressive credentials, it did not take long for this refined and attractive woman to became influential in local art circles. An authority on china painting, Oriental rugs, and antique furniture, she taught art-appreciation classes and gained recognition as the first interior decorator in Boise.

Marie Irvin painted in oils and watercolor, created prints, and designed wall coverings. Her graceful delicately brushed paper samples reflect her interest in historical decorative patterns, which she studied in New York. Irvin's still-life paintings are reminiscent of art nouveau fashion, while her neighborhood landscape scenes are rendered using soft tones in an impressionist style.

To her credit Marie Irvin provided a considerable service for the community during her thirty-four-year residence in Boise. She taught art at St. Margaret's School for Girls, was a leader in local organizations, became the state law librarian, and for more than twenty years was secretary and an active member of the Idaho Humane Society. She set standards for local art exhibits, assisted with a state-organized Chautauqua circuit and through her art and aesthetics classes "brought to many pioneer women their first knowledge and appreciation of art."[1]

1. *Idaho Daily Statesman* [Boise] 24 November 1968: 4C.

Born in Tennessee in 1876. Received diploma from Woman's School of Art, Cooper Union, New York; studied under muralist Robert Reid and with various art and architecture professors of the Boston Museum School of Art, New York University, Harvard, Columbia University, and the Chicago Art Institute. Came to Boise in 1898 to visit her father, the Boise City engineer. Became first art instructor at St. Margaret's School for Girls and also taught adult art classes. Served as state law librarian from December 1928, following the death of her sister Fanny who had held the office. Died in a Boise traffic accident March 2, 1932.

MARIE IRVIN
DESIGN FOR A RUG
CIRCA 1920s
WATERCOLOR ON PAPER
12 × 18"
COLLECTION COLLEGE OF IDAHO
ROSENTHAL GALLERY OF ART

SARA ANNETTE BOWMAN

Born in 1865. Educated at State Normal University, Normal, Illinois; School of Design, Davenport, Iowa; private lessons from sculptor Johann Gelert, Chicago, and wood carver Herr Behm of Vienna. Employed as assistant high school principal, Rock Island, Illinois; teacher of drawing, Illinois State Normal; supervisor of drawing, city schools of Tacoma, Washington; acting professor of art and design, University of Idaho, 1892-1901. Died in 1931.

Among the first four faculty members of the University of Idaho was an art instructor named Sara Annette Bowman. Educated in the Midwest, she held a number of positions in Illinois and Washington State before arriving in Moscow to teach at the University during the early 1890s.

At the turn of the century, Annette Bowman spent her summers painting in the countryside around Moscow and Lake Pend Oreille. During these visits to meadows and pastures, she sketched delicate floral studies of regional wildflowers. Bowman's watercolor renderings reveal that she was a careful observer of nature as well as a talented illustrator.

SARA ANNETTE BOWMAN
WILDFLOWER SKETCH
CIRCA 1904
10 × 7½"
COLLECTION UNIVERSITY OF IDAHO LIBRARY

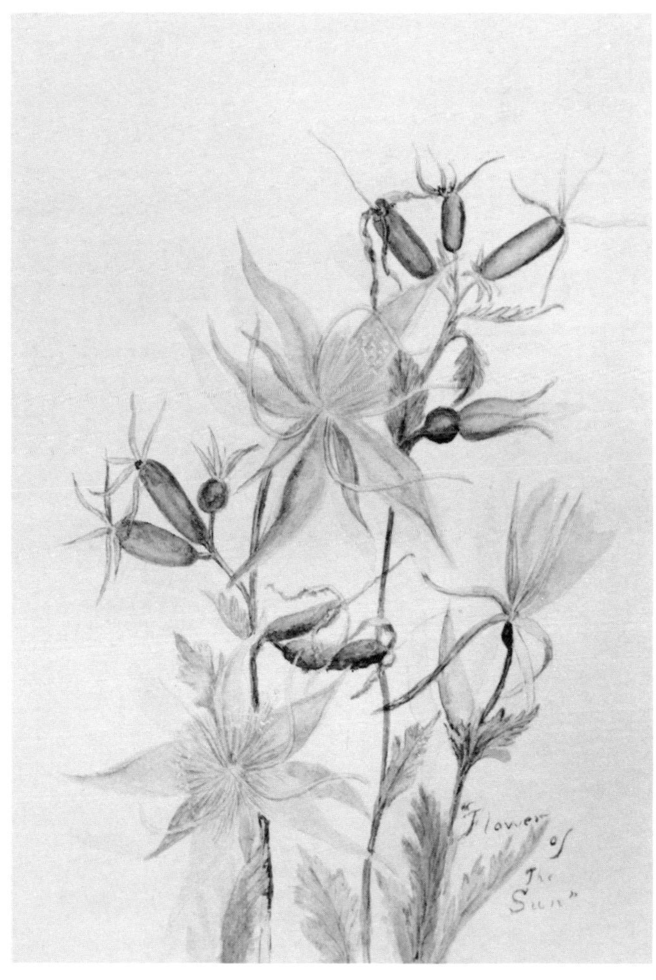

SARA ANNETTE BOWMAN
WILDFLOWER SKETCH
CIRCA 1904
WATERCOLOR ON PAPER
10 × 7½"
COLLECTION UNIVERSITY OF IDAHO LIBRARY

A STEP TOWARD PROGRESS

RICHARD GUY WALTON
SNAKE RIVER FERRY
1941
OIL ON CANVAS (MURAL)
U.S. POST OFFICE, BUHL, IDAHO
COURTESY JIM KOLVA

If early statehood years were difficult for aspiring artists, the war and depression years were even more challenging. Money was scarce, and professional artists, who found it hard to support themselves, were forced to seek other means of employment. Around the state there was no well-defined artistic milieu and no significant patronage. Although many amateur artists pursued artistic pastimes for pleasure, there were relatively few competitive exhibitions and virtually no professional art reviewers or critics. Local and state recognition was limited to the small circles of art clubs and occasional references in local newspapers. Yet even with these somewhat adverse conditions, there were positive forces within the state for arts education and cultural awareness.

Art instruction was first offered at a school of higher learning at the University of Idaho, which was founded in 1890. One of the initial four instructors at the university was Sara Annette Bowman, an artist who taught free-hand drawing. By the 1920s, art was part of the curriculum at Idaho State University and Gooding College, making art instruction more readily available to state residents. When ambitious local artists sought advanced training, they looked to eastern cities. It is surprising how many Idaho artists attended the Art Institute of Chicago and the Art Students League in New York, two of the best known art schools in the country. To complete their education, artists were often encouraged to study in Europe.

During the 1930s, the Federal Art Project, under the authority of the Works Projects Administration, offered an economic assistance program to American artists. In Idaho, the relief program directed by University of Idaho professor T. J. Prichard helped to employ seventeen artists. Although the projects were relatively small, the program furnished an important boost both economically and morally for delineators and sculptors. In the late 1930s, seven murals were commissioned for Idaho post offices. Themes ran along the line of pioneer settlement, wagon trains, and Indian campaigns, presenting visual narratives which celebrated romantic myths of the west. These narrative murals were designed to reach out to the public and impart an uplifting, optimistic spirit. Architectural commissions, although few, were also supported by the W.P.A. program. Noted artists such as Fletcher Martin and Vern Boven created decorative architectural elements for public buildings in Idaho.

In 1931, in order to meet a growing need, a group of interested Boise artists and citizens founded the Boise Art Association and sponsored the first Idaho Artists' Annual Exhibition, which became a statewide event for many years. Subsequently, the Boise Art Association proposed the construction of a gallery, and in 1937, under the auspices of the Works Project Administration, the Boise Gallery of Art became a permanent, bona fide exhibition space which hosted regional and national shows.

If an artistic style can be defined for the first half of the twentieth century in Idaho, the most notable factor is the influence of American and European Impressionism. Students who had attended the Chicago Art Institute and Art Students League had been exposed to the techniques of continental artists such as Monet, Van Gogh, and Cezanne, to name a few, and transformed their ideas into a brand of western American regionalist painting. Only toward mid-century did modern art theories of abstraction begin to make their influence felt. While western genre scenes, still lifes, and abstract artworks were in evidence at the time, landscapes, inspired by the grandeur of the mountains and the raw beauty which is Idaho, remained the predominant subject for art in the state.

From the time the first illustrators and artists came to Idaho until after World War II, the state had been, artistically speaking, a land of independent efforts created by touring artists, new arrivals and a peppering of native-born residents. When interpreted as a whole, their experiences and creative expressions provide a free-spirited artistic heritage and serve as a microcosm of Idaho history.

NELL SHIPMAN

NELL SHIPMAN
NELL SHIPMAN AS FAITH DIGGS
FINALE OF "THE GRUB STAKE"
ON LOCATION, THOROFARE,
PRIEST LAKE, IDAHO
1922
COURTESY HEMINGWAY WESTERN STUDIES CENTER, BSU

NELL SHIPMAN
NELL SHIPMAN COMPANY, LIONHEAD
LODGE, PRIEST LAKE, IDAHO
ON LOCATION, "THE LIGHT ON LOOKOUT"
1923-24
COURTESY HEMINGWAY WESTERN STUDIES CENTER, BSU

Born in Victoria, British Columbia, in 1892; moved to Seattle in 1902. Joined a vaudeville company at age 13 and toured the United States. Married Ernest Shipman, 1911. Wrote and starred in silent films in Hollywood and Canada, 1915-19. Lived and worked at Priest Lake, Idaho, 1922-25. Continued to write screenplays, documentaries, novels and short stories, 1930s-1960s. Completed her autobiography in 1969. Died in Cabazon, California, in 1970. Lionhead Park and Nell Shipman Point dedicated at Priest Lake, Idaho, August 31, 1977. Nell Shipman Festival held by Canadian Film Institute in 1974; Nell Shipman Silent Film Festival held by Boise State University, 1987.

Pioneer filmmaker and star, Nell Shipman was raised in a cultured middle-class family in the lush Canadian countryside of Vancouver Island. She was encouraged by her parents to read literature, be creative and enjoy the dramatic arts. As a teenager, she developed an interest in the performing arts and left home to join a theatrical company road show.

At eighteen, Nell married Ernest Shipman and moved to Southern California, where her husband worked in the motion picture field. She arrived in California in an era when talented women were influential in every aspect of film-making. Between 1912 and 1914, Shipman established her reputation as a scriptwriter, and in 1914 she wrote and directed three films for Universal Studios in which she also played the leading roles. Her success in the first feature-length wildlife adventure film, *God's Country and the Woman*, produced in 1915, launched Shipman's career as an independent producer-director.

Nell Shipman was ahead of her time. Rising above standard melodrama, her films are exceptional in their use of genuine wilderness locations and their portrayal of self-sufficient heroines. As a moviemaker she insisted on the humane treatment of animals, and her films underscore a sensitivity to nature. She also realized early on the value of independent production and collaborative film-making.

Determined to use authentic film locales, Shipman looked for a wilderness site to establish a production company, and in 1922 she moved from Hollywood to Idaho's Priest Lake. In what must have been a logistical nightmare, she transported over seventy animals, subjects of her films, to Lionhead Lodge, her lakeside studio in Priest River. Although rising costs of production forced her to close the studio in 1923, Nell Shipman's achievements in silent film were significant.

GEORGE EUGENE SCHROEDER

GEORGE SCHROEDER
MORNING BLUSH IN THE SAWTOOTHS
CIRCA 1920
OIL ON CANVAS
13½ × 35"
COLLECTION JOHN P. BLANCHARD

George Schroeder struggled with disability and adversity for much of his life, riding the highs and lows of success and failure. A frail child afflicted with acute curvature of the spine, Schroeder was bedridden during most of his youth and never attended school. Tutored by his cultured mother, he acquired a rudimentary education and developed an interest in literature and music.

As a young man, he apprenticed as a sign painter in Chicago, inscribing letters and images for commercial products. He moved to Omaha, where he developed a sign painting business so successful that branch offices were extended into four mid-western states. Sometime around 1905, "his fortunes were swept away by faith in others,"[1] and in 1906 Schroeder set out for Burley, Idaho, to begin a career in real estate. By 1914 he was again prosperous, owning a ranch six miles outside of Heyburn with fifty acres of lakes. Once more a prominent citizen, he opened his property to the Moorland Lakes Shooting Club for hunting and was mentioned in local newspapers as a city councilman as well as a director and stockholder in the Heyburn bank.

Following an unexplained change of events, Schroeder left Idaho, venturing to Europe to paint and study the old masters. Upon his return a year or so later, he led the meager life of a poor and struggling artist. He painted the rugged grandeur of mountains in southern Idaho, favoring the Sawtooths area. Working in oils, he specialized in romantic landscapes, influenced by French nineteenth-century painters he had studied in Europe.

With art as his primary interest and motivation, Schroeder endeavored to gain recognition in his craft. Persistent in his efforts to encourage development of art in southern Idaho, he worked to establish an art colony on Baker Creek near Ketchum, as well as an art center in Rupert for regional artists.

Of George Schroeder, it has been said: "Had he chosen the easier way, remained in the East and painted the West with colors of his imagination, George Schroeder would have been famous. But he chose the truer way and painted the West as it was and remained comparatively unsung and poor in the measure of golden treasure."[2]

1. *Idaho Teacher* December 1926:161.
2. *Golden Idaho Magazine* April 1934.

Born April 9, 1865, in Chicago; grew up in Oak Park, Illinois. Educated at home. Apprenticed to a Chicago sign painter. Moved to Omaha and operated a chain of sign-painting offices in Nebraska, Iowa, Missouri, and Kansas until 1906. Moved to Heyburn, Idaho, in 1906 and to Burley in 1912. Occupied as a landowner, bank director and real-estate agent in addition to painting. Painted scenes that decorated the Idaho "Governor's Special," a train that toured eastern states around 1914. Traveled and studied in Europe and New York. Maintained studios in Rupert and Heyburn in the 1920s; also lived briefly in Ogden, Utah. Taught young artists including Olaf Moller; promoted art training and an Idaho art collection. Died at his brother's home in Burley, April 13, 1934.

ROWENA ALCORN

Rowena Alcorn's fascination with Northwest Indians and regional history prompted her to document characters and scenes of early settlement days in Idaho. Born in Tacoma, Washington, she was educated at the University of Idaho in Moscow and lived in the northern panhandle during the 1930s. Rich in artistic accomplishments, Rowena Alcorn wrote ninety-six articles on Northwest and Indian history, taught painting for twenty-eight years, and is known throughout the Northwest for her depiction of Nez Perce Indians and events related to their history.

Alcorn took great care to represent historical events accurately; she thoroughly researched topics and story elements. When possible, she interviewed friends or relatives of subjects to be portrayed in order to gain accurate physical descriptions and insight into character. For depictions of historic buildings, she used original plans and on-site sketches to guarantee authenticity.

A well-known figure painted by Rowena Alcorn is Idaho's first missionary, Henry Harmon Spalding. Painted in an impressionist style, he appears as a stern patriarch. Spalding traveled overland by wagon with his wife and another missionary couple, Marcus and Narcissa Whitman, in 1836. These early missionaries, sponsored by eastern Presbyterians and Congregationalists, came in response to requests by the Nez Perce Indians. The Spaldings established a mission in 1836 at Lapwai, twelve miles from Lewiston, and there the family remained for eleven years. To Spalding's credit, he initiated farming, opened a grist mill, built a school for Indian children and operated the first printing press in the Northwest.

Born March 27, 1905, in Tacoma, Washington. Educated at University of Idaho; State Teachers College and School of Arts, Santa Barbara, California. Studied under several members of the National Academy of Design. Director of Armstrong School of Art, Tacoma, 1928-35; and instructor of painting at College of Puget Sound, 1930-35. Married professor of botany Dr. Gordon D. Alcorn in 1935, and returned to Moscow, Idaho, in the late 1930s. Head of art department, Grays Harbor Junior College, 1940s. Taught twenty-eight years as part time art instructor. Exhibited throughout the United States. Works in private and public collections throughout Northwest.

ELIZA SPALDING
ARRIVAL OF THE WHITMAN-SPALDING PARTY AT THE SUMMIT OF THE ROCKIES
COPY BY UNKNOWN ARTIST
N.D.
OIL ON CANVAS.
9½ × 13½"
HENRY AND ELIZA SPALDING PAPERS
COLLECTION WASHINGTON STATE UNIVERSITY LIBRARIES

Initial efforts by missionaries to settle in Idaho failed. Spalding's cantankerous nature led him to quarrel with whites, non-whites and missionaries sent to assist his efforts. Whitman, who established a mission at Waiilatpu on the Walla Walla River, in Washington Territory, was massacred by the Cayuse Indians in 1847. Spalding's difficult personality and inability to get along, coupled with Indian unrest in the area, forced him to leave Lapwai. Rowena Alcorn's portrait of Spalding was used as the frontispiece of Clifford Drury's 1936 biography of the missionary.

Rowena Alcorn focused on Nez Perce history because it was a neglected subject compared to research on other Native American groups. In a project that took twenty years to execute, she painted a series of Nez Perce Indian portraits at Lapwai, twelve of which were exhibited in Tacoma and Seattle in 1936. Today, Rowena Alcorn is recognized as the first modern artist to paint the historically significant Nez Perce tribe.

ROWENA ALCORN
PORTRAIT OF HENRY HARMON SPALDING
1936
OIL ON CANVAS
31⅝ × 23⅜"
COLLECTION NEZ PERCE NATIONAL HISTORICAL PARK
NATIONAL PARK SERVICE

KATHERINE JOY POSTLE

KATHERINE POSTLE
THE MALAD CANYON
CIRCA 1925
OIL ON PANEL
25¼ × 35¼"
COLLECTION BOISE ART MUSEUM

Born January 20, 1896, in Chicago. Attended Art Institute of Chicago. Taught at St. Margaret's School, Boise. Painted portraits, murals; recognized for her landscapes of Snake River Country in the mid-1920s. Married Robert Blackstone and moved in 1929 to the South. Studied and sketched indigenous Florida waterfowl during 1930s; produced and presented "Glamour Birds," an original act presented in southern states.

During her ten-year residence in Idaho, Katherine Postle lived on a ranch overlooking the Snake River Canyon. A plein air landscape painter, she had a special affinity for the rugged canyons and desert scenes of southern Idaho. She often rode on horseback into the desert or hills to sketch. *Malad Canyon*, painted around 1925, presents a dramatic view from atop the canyon's rock walls, overlooking the gorge 250 feet below. Postle's impressionist painting style was most likely influenced by the formal training she received at the Chicago Art Institute.

In the late 1920s, Postle married and moved with her husband to Pensacola, Florida. In 1934, her career took a decided turn when she began to specialize in painting "wading birds" of the Deep South. She sloshed through marshes to snatch intimate sketches of flamingos, egrets, ibises, and spoonbills nesting with their young or feeding in swamplands. After five years studying birds in their native habitats, she developed a career as a "performing" artist. Her entertaining repartee included songs, witty stories, and original verse which she recited as she drew colorful life-size wading birds. "Glamour Birds," as her act was billed, received glowing comments and praise as authentic entertainment from the naturalist's point of view.

BENJAMIN CHAMBERS BROWN

BENJAMIN CHAMBERS BROWN
RED FISH LAKE, IDAHO
CIRCA 1900-1940
OIL ON CANVAS
48 × 60"
COLLECTION BOISE PUBLIC LIBRARY

Benjamin Chambers Brown was a midwesterner from St. Louis who traveled to Europe as a student during the 1880s and attended the Academie Julian in Paris. He went to Europe at a time when the impressionist style was popular and numerous works by prominent French artists were on display in galleries and salons. Brown, like many artists studying in Paris, was drawn to Impressionism because it offered a fresh approach to visual problems and freed contemporary painting from the restrictiveness of academic taste and formula.

Upon Brown's return to the United States, he adapted his technical skills to painting the western landscape. In his depiction of *Redfish Lake*, he incorporated impressionist color theories and techniques. This large-scale painting's immediacy and spontaneity are due to Brown's sophisticated use of rapid brushwork; each stroke catches the momentary color and stresses the effects of natural light. The "snapshot" composition of the painting reflects not only the influence of impressionist concepts, but also the artist's study of photography early in his life. Brown, who lived in California for nearly fifty years, toured and painted in the Northwest around 1910. His large-scale mountain scenes and landscapes brought him national acclaim.

Born in Marion, Arkansas, on July 14, 1865. Trained as a photographer, studied at St. Louis School of Fine Art and Academie Julian, Paris. Specialized in portraiture and still life while in Missouri, Arkansas, and Texas. Moved to Pasadena, California, in 1896. Focused on landscape painting; began etching in 1914. Recipient of many awards in West Coast expositions; works held in major museums across the U.S. Died January 19, 1942.

NICK VILLENEUVE

Idaho's premier cartoonist, Nick Villeneuve was a jovial character and entertaining personality. During the era of World War I, he expressed his wit and humor in editorial cartoons produced for the *Idaho Daily Statesman*. Villeneuve caricatures jabbed at influential state politicians and took aim at national public figures.

Villeneuve was born and raised in the Boise Valley. Aside from three months when he received instruction at the Chicago Art Institute in 1902, he lived in Idaho throughout his life. Villeneuve's humorous characterizations first came to public attention while he was working for *Illustrated Idaho*, a monthly publication which promoted the state. In the early 1910s, he was hired by the *Idaho Daily Statesman* as their first local cartoonist. His caricatures were regularly featured on the front page before and during World War I. A prolific artist, he produced over 500 pen-and-ink drawings as well as 500 engraver's plates during his career. The majority of these works employ a down-to-earth approach influenced by the art styles of Norman Rockwell and N. C. Wyeth, whose work Villeneuve admired.

In addition to creating editorial cartoons for the newspaper, Villeneuve was employed in 1926 by Idaho Power Company to produce promotional and advertising art. Most Idahoans are familiar with the company's logo, "Reddy Kilowatt," a cartoon figure that he created. In 1938 he collaborated on and illustrated a tongue-in-cheek book of poems and stories based on imaginary Idaho creatures, entitled *A Saga of the Sawtooths*. Reaching a larger audience, his illustrations appeared in publications such as the *New York World* and *Literary Digest*.

Although Villeneuve made his living at the drawing board, he aspired to be on stage; in local amateur productions, he acted, sang, and danced. His boundless curiosity and gregarious nature made him a well-liked personality. For over forty years, Villenueve shared his insights on politicians and commented on current events in cartoons which amused Idahoans and earned him a national reputation.

Born in the Boise Valley, October 23, 1883. Studied at Art Institute of Chicago, 1902. Worked as editorial cartoonist for the Idaho Daily Statesman; *W.W. I cartoons published in book form. Employed by Idaho Power as illustrator-draftsman beginning in 1926. Published* Saga of the Sawtooths *with Henry Senger, 1938. One-man show at Boise Art Gallery, 1938, and a retrospective at the Idaho State Historical Museum, 1986. Died in 1947. Works in the collection of Idaho State Historical Society and Huntington Library, San Marino, California.*

NICK VILLENEUVE
IDAHO'S GRAND OLD MAN
1923
WATERCOLOR AND INK ON PAPER
27½ × 19½"
COLLECTION IDAHO STATE HISTORICAL SOCIETY

HERBERT MORTON STOOPS

Born in Idaho in 1887; grew up on a ranch west of Yellowstone Park. Graduate of Utah State College; studied at Art Institute of Chicago. Worked as artist-reporter for the San Francisco Call, 1910, *and as staff artist for the* Chicago Tribune. *Served in World War I as an artillery officer in France. Settled in New York City. Exhibited at National Academy of Design, 1940. Sometimes signed work with pseudonyms "Jeremy Cannon" and "Raymond Sisley." Died at Mystic, Connecticut, May 19, 1948.*

Herbert Morton Stoops was born on a ranch in central Idaho's mountains in 1888. As a youth he worked as a cowhand and learned the stockman's trade by handling horses and cattle. From older wranglers he heard accounts of adventures on the frontier plains and firsthand tales of Indian Wars. These stories colored his imagination, and his boyhood memories strongly influenced his future career.

At the behest of his clergyman father, Stoops left the ranch to study at Utah State College. After his graduation he ventured to the Pacific Coast to became an artist-reporter for the *San Francisco Call* newspaper around 1910. At that time San Francisco was the focal point for important western illustrators, and Stoops was afforded the opportunity to see the work of such popular contemporary artists as Maynard Dixon. Spurred to advance his career and education, Stoops moved to Chicago and worked for the *Chicago Tribune*, concurrently attending classes at the Chicago Art Institute.

During the 1920s, Stoops gained a reputation as an important illustrator in the tradition of Frederic Remington. As a commercial artist, Stoops illustrated magazines, notably *Collier's* and *Cosmopolitan*, as well as books specializing in the Old West and military subjects. He was particularly known for his western scenes, which he derived from his early experiences in Idaho. Whether painting the workaday world of the cowboy or interpreting historic events, he brought to life the excitement of the West and its people.

HERBERT MORTON STOOPS
CONFRONTATION
CIRCA 1920s
OIL ON CANVAS
32 × 36"
COURTESY SIDESTREET GALLERY, SANDPOINT, IDAHO

CECIL ALDEN SMITH

CECIL SMITH
A LITTLE MIXUP
1939
DRY BRUSH ON PAPER
10¾ × 20"
COLLECTION BOISE ART MUSEUM

Born February 12, 1910, in Salt Lake City. Raised on a ranch at Carey, Idaho. Educated at University of Utah, Brigham Young University; studied journalism at University of Hawaii; studied art at Chicago Art Institute and in New York. Worked as a cowboy throughout the West. Participated in Idaho WPA artists' program, 1930s. Served in the U.S. Navy during World War II. Visited Australia, 1950-52. Worked as freelance artist and illustrator and as art director for various organizations. Moved to Somers, Montana; died at Kalispell November 6, 1984. Exhibited widely, received recognition in U.S. and abroad; subject of many articles in Western magazines and newspapers. Works in numerous private and public collections, including 30 murals at the BYU motion picture studio, Provo, Utah.

Cecil Smith believed that no artist was a true "cowboy artist" unless he earned his living as a working cattleman. Smith was a native of Idaho whose grandfather was among the first to settle in the Little Wood River country of central Idaho in the 1880s. His ranch, the 89,000-acre Bar Bell Land and Cattle Company, was the largest single block of deeded land in the state.

Smith was groomed from childhood to enter the ranching business, but his mother saw to it that he also cultivated his talent for painting. With encouragement, he attended Brigham Young University and University of Utah. Summers he spent working as a cowpuncher on the open grass range; from the saddle and by the campfire, Smith prepared hundreds of sketches of cowboy life.

Early in his career he painted *Twenty Mule Team*, which describes mining days in the Ketchum area when ore and provisions were freighted between the Salmon River and the nearest smelter kilns in Kelton, Utah. To develop the image, Smith drew from first-hand experience. For many years his father had worked as a freighter and muleskinner for Horres Lewis of Ketchum. Lewis, who is remembered in the area for constructing the Trail Creek Grade and the Galena Summit Road, owned many wagon outfits similar to the one portrayed in the painting. *Twenty Mule Team* was commissioned by the Idaho

CECIL SMITH
TWENTY MULE TEAM
1934
OIL ON CANVAS
25 × 48"
COLLECTION IDAHO STATE HISTORICAL SOCIETY

Department of Mines during the 1930s under the auspices of the Works Progress Administration, President Roosevelt's experimental employment program, a portion of which provided help to artists caught in the economic doldrums of the Depression.

At age twenty-nine Smith traveled to New York, where he studied with modernists John Carroll, Max Weber and Yasuo Kuniyoshi. He recalls, "I was taught to paint realistically, to try to portray the true character and texture of my subject."[1] Cecil Smith's painting career was interrupted by World War II, but following the war, he returned home to devote his time to painting and running the Bar Bell Ranch.

Throughout his life Smith found fulfillment combining what he was born and raised to do with what he wanted to do. The Bar Bell ranch was sold in 1956, relieving Smith of ranching duties and allowing him to paint with devoted and undivided interest. Of his work Smith states: "What feeling I am able to project comes from my very strong connection with the things I paint...I have experienced the places and the action...I'll hear the wind or watch it bend the grass and that observation will give me a feeling of some long ago experience which is replayed in my work."[2]

1. Weedon, M. V. "Cecil Smith, Last of the Rare Breed: Cowboy Artists." *Western Horseman* January 1977:7.
2. Oliveria, David F. "A Rare Breed of Artist." *Southwest Art* February 1978:55.

MINERVA TEICHERT

The daughter of covered-wagon pioneers, Minerva Kohlhepp Teichert was raised on an isolated farm near American Falls, Idaho. Talented and compelled to paint, she taught school in eastern Idaho to earn tuition to attend the Chicago Art Institute. Upon completion of a four-year program, she was awarded a scholarship in 1914 to work under the influential American artist Robert Henri at the Art Students League in New York.

After several years in the city and at a crucial point in her education, she found that "there was too much sagebrush in my blood to forget the beauties of rugged mountains, dry plains and wonderful atmosphere."[1] Giving up an opportunity to study in London, she returned to Idaho to marry her cowboy sweetheart. Settling in what is referred to as the "bottoms" of the Fort Hall Indian Reservation near American Falls, she became a ranch wife and raised five children. Unfortunately, their home was in lands designated to be inundated by the creation of American Falls Reservoir, and the family relocated to Cokeville, Wyoming, just across the state line.

It was the scrub country of the "bottoms," however, which inspired her imagination and greatly influenced her art and writings. In numerous paintings and several books, she preserved memories of her life in the lowlands along the shores of the Snake River.

For the most part, Teichert's paintings are nostalgic evocations of western scenes, often replete with pioneers and cattle. In *Ox Drawn Wagon Fording Creek*, large sweeping figures dominate the canvas. As in a great majority of her works, there is a suggestion of motion, here implied by the forward movement of lumbering oxen straining to pull a prairie schooner up an embankment. Teichert's ease and familiarity with large-scale narrative subjects made her an able candidate to create murals for several regional Mormon churches. A devoted member of the church, she worked for nearly half a century to chronicle episodes from the *Book of Mormon* and to reflect through heroic characters the religious values of the church. Teichert's life work includes over one thousand scenes, murals, and florals, illustrating Mormon history and western subjects.

1. *Idaho State Journal* 22 July 1988: 12C.

Born August 28, 1888, at North Ogden, Utah. Graduate of Pocatello High School, 1906. Studied at Art Institute of Chicago, 1908-12; studied with Robert Henri at the Art Students League, 1914-17. Protegee of Dr. Minnie Howard, Idaho state arts administrator. Married Herman Teichert in 1917 and raised a family in the Fort Hall Bottoms near American Falls. Moved permanently to Cokeville, Wyoming, in 1927. Published Drowned Memories (1926), Romance of Old Fort Hall (1932). *Died May 3, 1976. Works in many* LDS *temples and schools; public buildings in Idaho and Utah; the Start Collection, Austin, Texas; Brigham Young University; Museum of Church History and Art, Salt Lake City.*

MINERVA TEICHERT
OX DRAWN WAGON FORDING CREEK
CIRCA 1940
OIL ON CANVAS
18½ × 48"
IDAHO STATE UNIVERSITY
STUDENT UNION PERMANENT ART COLLECTION

HELEN HOFF AUPPERLE

Born October 25, 1905, in Idaho Falls. Attended Chouinard School of Art, Los Angeles. B.A., 1930, University of California, Los Angeles; M.A., Claremont Graduate School, Claremont, California, 1966. Further study at Royal Academy of Art, Stockholm, and Royal Academy of Art, Copenhagen. Taught in Long Beach, California, 1930-1939. Married Don Aupperle, 1940. Initiated curriculum and taught high school art classes in Idaho Falls, 1946-1969. Recipient of national Outstanding Teacher Award, 1966. Co-founder of Idaho Falls Art Guild and Idaho Art Association. Died February 1971. One-woman exhibits at Charles Russell Gallery in Helena, Montana, University of Idaho, Idaho State University, Ricks College, College of Idaho, Boise Gallery of Art; represented annually in Idaho artists shows at Boise Gallery of Art, 1940s-1960s. Retrospective exhibit in 1971 at Idaho State Historical Museum and First Security Bank, Idaho Falls.

"To thousands of people in eastern Idaho, Helen Hoff Aupperle was synonymous with creativity. She made people aware of art as a vital enrichment to life, both through her teaching and personal involvement in many other activities."[1] A native of Idaho, Helen Aupperle was raised on a farm southeast of Idaho Falls. When she was young, her father became ill and they moved to southern California, where she attended high school and later graduated from University of California, Los Angeles. She began her teaching career with a ten-year tenure at Long Beach Polytechnic high school, followed by a year's sabbatical at leading art institutions in Denmark and Sweden. Upon completion of her European training, she returned to Idaho Falls, and through her devotion to teaching and talent for art, she gained the admiration of the community.

Around 1939, Aupperle began regularly visiting the Shoshone-Bannock Reservation and quickly became intrigued with Indian festivals, dances, and ceremonies. With sketch pad in hand, Aupperle began drawing the local residents in their native dress. Her initial interest in describing the people heightened as she became aware that the Bannock and Shoshone traditions and culture were gradually being lost.

Frequently returning to sketch at Fort Hall, Aupperle soon won the respect of tribal members. Typical of her work is the portrait of *Willie George*, dressed in ceremonial garb and wearing the chief's headdress. Willie George, a respected leader of the Shoshone tribe, was proud of his heritage and advocated preserving the Indian way of life. He wore his hair in long braids and often dressed in Shoshone costume when performing as a rodeo star.

Aupperle, who taught school in Idaho Falls High School for twenty-two years, was not only a talented artist, but had a special ability to impart her knowledge and enthusiasm for art to others. In 1966, she was one of twenty-five American teachers to receive a National Gallery of Art award from President Lyndon Johnson at the White House for her distinguished service to arts education.

1. Hart, Arthur. "Painter of Idaho Indians." *Incredible Idaho* Fall 1971: 14.

HELEN HOFF AUPPERLE
"RUNNING BEAR"—WILLIE GEORGE
CIRCA 1940
OIL ON CANVAS
48 × 36"
COLLECTION DON AUPPERLE

OSCAR OLAF MOLLER

OLAF MOLLER
UNION PACIFIC DEPOT
1934
OIL ON CANVAS
20 × 24"
COLLECTION BOISE ART MUSEUM

Born May 21, 1903, in Aarhus, Denmark. Brought to America at six months; lived in Brooklyn, Montana, Salt Lake City, and Boise. Moved in 1912 to a homestead between Rupert and Paul, Idaho. Took art lessons from George Schroeder in Paul. Attended Pennsylvania Academy of Fine Arts, 1921-1929. Received a scholarship to the Louis Comfort Tiffany Foundation. Returned to Rupert in 1929. Participated in the WPA artists' program, 1930s. Taught painting and constructed custom frames for over forty years. Died in Boise, 1985. Exhibited at Springville, Heyburn, Salt Lake City in the 1930s; Boise Art Gallery, 1938; New York World's Fair, 1940; and in many galleries in the Eastern United States. Retrospective shows at Springville Museum of Art, 1978, and at the Nordic Heritage Museum, Seattle, 1987.

Olaf Moller was a self-proclaimed "realist" who disavowed abstract art. He strove to attain a likeness so beautifully real that the viewer would want to step inside the picture: "I like realism, I try to make it as real as I can. I like people to say, 'I want to go hunting, fishing or camping in there.'"[1] Unlike many painters who romanticized the West, Moller preferred the West as it actually was.

Moller's parents were Danish immigrants who left their homeland in 1903 to seek a better life in the American Far West. Tenacious individuals, they made the long trek first to Montana and then to Utah before taking up the challenge of homesteading eighty acres on the expansive Snake River Plain. One of eight children, Olaf was expected to work on the family farm, but his talent for art opened doors and provided opportunities. He submitted a painting and was accepted to the Pennsylvania Academy of Art, where he had the good fortune to study under N. C. Wyeth. After eight years of the "best training," Moller was headed towards a successful career, but as the Depression years began, Moller found it necessary to return to Idaho.

Moller lived to paint and spent much of his time in the outdoors. He often went on summer outings with his friend Archie Teater, a well-known artist from nearby Hagerman, to paint their favorite mountain scenery in the Sawtooths and the Tetons. On occasion he strayed from traditional landscapes, as in *The Union Pacific Station*, which was commissioned for presentation to Joel Priest, a Union Pacific man instrumental in bringing the main railroad line to Boise.

With the exception of several sojourns in New England, Moller remained to the end of his life in the Rupert/Paul area. A frequent exhibitor, recipient of many awards, and active art instructor, he considered himself fortunate in being able to earn his living as an artist in Idaho.

1. *Times-News* [Twin Falls, Idaho] 15 Feb. 1980: 3.

FANNY DIKE BURNS

FANNY DIKE BURNS
MUSTARD FIELD
1935
OIL ON CANVAS
11¾ × 17½"
COLLECTION BOISE ART MUSEUM

Fanny Dike Burns was instrumental in organizing the first permanent art association in southern Idaho. Through her persistent efforts during the early 1930s, she helped establish the Boise Art Association which became the Boise Gallery of Art and is now the Boise Art Museum.

Originally from Illinois, Burns attended the Chicago Art Institute prior to coming to Idaho with her husband in 1924. Eager to bring culture and an understanding of fine arts to Boise, she actively promoted the establishment of a cultural organization; and by 1931, Burns' proposal for an art association became a reality. She established a committee to draft a constitution and by-laws and served as the first vice president and membership chairman in 1934. Soon thereafter, she pursued the possibility of building an exhibition space, and through her endeavors, the city's Park Board provided land in Julia Davis Park. Subsequently, the Boise Gallery of Art was constructed and opened its doors to the public in 1937. Serving on the board of trustees, Burns set in motion a series of programs which included visiting lecturers and classes with local craftsmen.

A printmaker and painter, Fanny Burns joined a local artists' group to sketch scenes in Boise Basin and the surrounding region. Her painting *Mustard Field* won first prize in the first annual Artists of Idaho Exhibition, 1935. Its bright sunny colors dabbled with impasto reflect her art school training at the Chicago Art Institute, where she assimilated impressionist techniques. In both her roles, as painter and as arts advocate, Fanny Dike Burns devoted her talents to the benefit of Boise, enabling the community to enjoy and appreciate the fine arts.

Born in Chicago, Illinois, in 1885. Studied at Chicago Art Institute and Chicago Academy of Fine Arts, and taught in the Chicago school system. Married Willard W. Burns and moved to Boise in 1924. Exhibited at Boise and Heyburn, Idaho. Died in 1962.

JAMES CASTLE

James Castle never heard nor ever spoke a word. He was born deaf in Garden Valley, Idaho, in 1900. He did not learn to read, write, or use sign language; his only means of communication was visual. He began drawing as a child and continued throughout his life. Although he had no formal art training or exposure to fine arts, his work reveals an unusual perception and imagination, inspired by purely visual responses to his immediate environment.

Castle used his art to make sense of his world. From a very early age, he drew interiors of his home, farm buildings, human figures, and fantasy landscapes. The majority of Castle's works are small and include drawings, assemblages and books. Sketches were made on scraps of paper and cardboard with unorthodox materials such as chimney soot for ink and old cardboard cartons for drawing surfaces; Castle scorned traditional drawing materials in favor of homemade ones. Created from what was at hand, the drawings took on a rustic quality which enhanced each image.

James Castle imparts an ominous and quiet drama to his interpretation of everyday objects and scenes. The drawings are beautifully rendered, demonstrating a sophisticated approach to space and a wide range of tonality. Their powerful impact is due to a strong impression of mood. Landscapes and rooms are absent of activity, evoking an environment of loneliness.

Born September 25, 1900, in Garden Valley, Idaho. Occasionally attended Gooding School for the Blind and Deaf. Lived with his family in Garden Valley, where his father was postmaster and owner of the general store, until 1920. Moved to Star, and to Boise in 1929; lived with his younger sister after his mother's death in 1948. Died October 27, 1977. Exhibitions at the Portland Museum Art School (1951), Monmouth, Oregon (1960), Image Gallery, Portland, and Salem Art Museum (1962), California College of Arts and Crafts, Oakland (1965), Bellevue, Wash., and Salt Lake Art Center in the 1960s, College of Idaho (1969), Ochi Gallery, Boise (1976), Washington State University and Foster/White Gallery, Seattle (1974), Art Museum of South Texas (1981); a show organized by the Boise Gallery of Art in 1982 traveled to six western locations.

JAMES CASTLE
WOOD STOVE
N.D.
CHARCOAL AND SOOT ON CARDBOARD
8 × 8"
COLLECTION BOISE ART MUSEUM

Most unusual are the drawings and calendars assembled into book format. Castle produced numerous small books composed from scraps of paper torn to size and bound with string. Generally of two kinds, calendars and picture books, these pages of endless invention are filled with mysterious shapes, signs, and symbols. Pages held at least one illustration and in most cases appeared in photo album style with many small pictures accompanied by wavy lines scribbled underneath to indicate an unknown personal narrative.

In the course of a life devoted to drawing, James Castle raised, pursued, and solved many problems of representation which have intrigued all artists. The essence of James Castle's talent is the successful resolution of these questions. Neither naive nor primitive, James Castle's art shows startling visual awareness. Castle, who died in 1977, was essentially a private person who projected his view of the world with great sensitivity and perception.

JAMES CASTLE
YARD WITH FANTASY FORMS
N.D.
CHARCOAL, SOOT, AND WATER ON PAPER
$6\frac{3}{4} \times 8\frac{7}{16}$"
COLLECTION BOISE ART MUSEUM

ETHEL LUCILE FOWLER

ETHEL FOWLER
FATHER
1933
WATERCOLOR ON PAPER
10 × 8"
COLLECTION BOISE ART MUSEUM

Born in Juniata, Nebraska. Studied at Pennsylvania School of Industrial Art, Chicago Art Institute, Chouinard Art Institute, Los Angeles; and with several private instructors. Awards at Lewis & Clark Exposition, Portland, 1905; Idaho State Fairs 1904-1916; Boise Gallery of Art annual Idaho artists' exhibitions. Work shown in National Exhibition of American Art, New York, 1937. Participated in Idaho Public Works of Art Project, 1930s. Works in the Boise Art Museum and private collections.

Ethel Fowler was a highly regarded Boise artist who exhibited with the Boise Art Association in its early days. Her firsthand knowledge of art was gained through studies at opposite ends of the country. She first attended the Chicago Art Institute, then the Pennsylvania School of Industrial Art in Philadelphia, and refined her techniques at the Chouinard Art Institute in Los Angeles.

During the more than thirty years that Fowler lived in Idaho, her reputation as a portrait painter and an art teacher quietly grew. She was also known for numerous delicate watercolors of local scenery, flowers, and still lifes. Typical of her work is this expressive watercolor of her father painted in 1933.

AGNES RANDALL MOORE

AGNES RANDALL MOORE
TWO WOMEN IN SUITS
CIRCA 1930
INK ON MATBOARD
10½ × 8"
COLLECTION LATAH COUNTY HISTORICAL SOCIETY

Agnes Randall Moore descended from pioneers who homesteaded the area southwest of Moscow, Idaho, during the nineteenth century. She grew up on the family farm nestled in the rolling hills which surround the University. Moore's interest in art began as a youngster, and like many of her peers, she attended the University of Idaho. Following graduation, Moore furthered her education by studying at the Chicago Art Institute.

Moore's black and white representational drawings, which are characterized by the strong use of positive-negative space, sketched in pen and ink, were well suited for book illustration. Consequently, she was hired to illustrate a series of children's stories written by Ruth Plowhead and published by Caxton Printers of Caldwell. She is remembered as a distinguished western illustrator and painter.

Born October 24, 1905, near Moscow, Idaho. Educated at the Ursuline Academy, Moscow; Chicago Art Institute; B.A., 1930 and M.A., 1936, University of Idaho. Taught at University of Idaho, 1931-32; at the Ursuline Convent, Moscow public schools, and at Long Pine and Fern Dell rural schools. Illustrated Lucretia Ann *children's books published in 1930s and in 1955. Married William Cloud Moore in 1933 and raised a family; returned to painting in the 1960s. Exhibited in several one-woman shows; works owned by public agencies and private collectors. Died February 12, 1977, at Moscow.*

NELLIE KILGORE KLINGE

Originally from Illinois, Nellie Kilgore Klinge attended two of the country's most prestigious art schools, the Chicago Art Institute and Pratt Institute in New York. Little of her life is known other than she came west to Colorado where she taught at a junior high school in Denver and at Colorado State College in Fort Collins. While living in Colorado she also worked as a designer of stained glass for the Denver company, McPhee and McGinnity.

It is uncertain when she moved to Idaho, but the majority of her paintings are landscapes, florals and portraits of local subjects. She is quoted as saying, "The locale of my painting has been mostly in southeastern Idaho. In my work I endeavor to express the beauty and charm of a scene in a virile, rhythmic composition."[1] As one of the first artists to be presented by the newly founded Boise Art Association, she exhibited the still life *Zinnias* in 1933.

1. *The Idaho Encyclopedia* (Caldwell, Idaho: Caxton Printers, 1938) 174.

Born in Marshall, Illinois. Graduate of Colorado State College, Ft. Collins; studied at Chicago Art Institute, Pratt Institute, Brooklyn School of Fine & Applied Arts, and Utah State Agricultural College, Logan. Exhibited frequently with Springville (Utah), Heyburn, and Boise Art Associations in the 1930s while living in Preston, Idaho. Paintings in Heyburn and Kimberly, Idaho, high schools; Boise Art Museum.

NELLIE KILGORE KLINGE
ZINNIAS
1937
OIL ON PANEL
28 × 21"
COLLECTION BOISE ART MUSEUM

CORNELIA HART FARRER

Born July 31, 1889 in Boise, Idaho. Graduate of Boise High School and Chicago Academy of Fine Arts. Further study at University of Washington, Pedro Lemos School in Palo Alto, California, and Delacleuse School in Paris. Taught art in her Boise studio and helped initiate Music Week. Traveled and sketched in France and Italy, then taught in Tulsa, Oklahoma. Returned to Boise in the 1930s and managed the art department of The Mode department store. Married Vern Farrer in 1941. A founding member and past president of the Boise Art Association, board member of the Beaux Arts Societe. Published stories; exhibited in National Exhibition of American Art, New York, 1937, and with the Boise Art Association. Currently resides in Boise.

Cornelia Hart Farrer, a native of Boise, was involved for many years in artistic and aesthetic projects in the capitol city. As a young woman, she attended the Chicago Academy of Fine Arts and upon graduation spent several months in Paris studying painting and absorbing European culture. In the early 1920s, Cornelia taught art at St. Margaret's Academy in Boise and later opened a studio for art classes. Always a promoter of culture for Boise, Cornelia worked toward establishing an art gallery in Julia Davis Park as one of the founding members of the Boise Art Association.

An active painter, Cornelia Hart Farrer participated in a group of local Boiseans who called themselves the "Ho Bohemians." This fun-loving band of six or more artists toured the hills of the surrounding region looking for picturesque sights to paint. They could frequently be seen in the pioneer mining town Idaho City, considered a good place for local artists to find colorful subjects and interesting architecture. Their work, mainly landscapes in oil and pastels, was exhibited at various locations about town; the Hill House restaurant, the Carnegie Library, the First National Bank were popular places to display.

Beginning in 1930 Cornelia took over the management of a local retail store art department, lending her services by designing art work for specialty items. For clientele at The Mode, she hand-decorated screens, lamp shades and household objects. It was affectionately said that, "Cornelia Hart — she daubed up everything in Boise." A vibrant sunny personality, Cornelia Hart Farrer championed many causes for the arts and the preservation of historic sites in Boise and around the state.

CORNELIA HART FARRER
PEACEFUL COVE
CIRCA 1950
OIL ON BOARD
23¾ × 17¾"
COLLECTION IDAHO CITY HISTORICAL FOUNDATION, INC.

REEVES EULER

REEVES EULER
HEAD OF A WOMAN
1947
SANDSTONE SCULPTURE
21½ × 11 × 8"
COLLECTION BOISE ART MUSEUM

Born December 28, 1896, in De Lamar, Nevada. Graduated from Boise High School in 1916; moved east in 1917. Studied at Corcoran School of Art, Washington, D.C., National Academy of Design, New York, and with Charles W. Hawthorne, Provincetown, Mass. Exhibited in Corcoran Biennial 1935, 1937, 1939; Phillips Collection, National Academy of Design, National Gallery, Washington; and numerous other East Coast museums and traveling shows. One-man exhibit at Boise Art Gallery, 1938.

Reeves Euler descended from pioneers who came west over the plains on their way to California. After several years on the coast, his forebears went to Boise in 1866 and established residence in Silver City during the boomtown's early days. Euler's father became associated with Captain De Lamar of mining fame, and the family was moved to De Lamar, Nevada, the site of Euler's birth in 1896. After several years, the family relocated to Nampa, Idaho, where Euler spent most of his childhood. He studied at two distinguished institutions, the Corcoran Gallery of Art in Washington, D.C., and the National Academy of Design in New York. Euler became a well-established and successful artist who resided mainly in Provincetown, Massachusetts, for most of his career.

In 1938, Euler came back to Idaho and exhibited a selection of work at the newly constructed Boise Gallery of Art. The body of this show consisted of local scenes, landscapes of Boise Valley, and views of Payette Lake. In many later works, he also created highly-stylized images, including sandstone portrait sculptures. This Idaho artist, who achieved national distinction for his work, was shown in many significant exhibitions and his art was purchased for numerous private collections in the East.

FLETCHER MARTIN

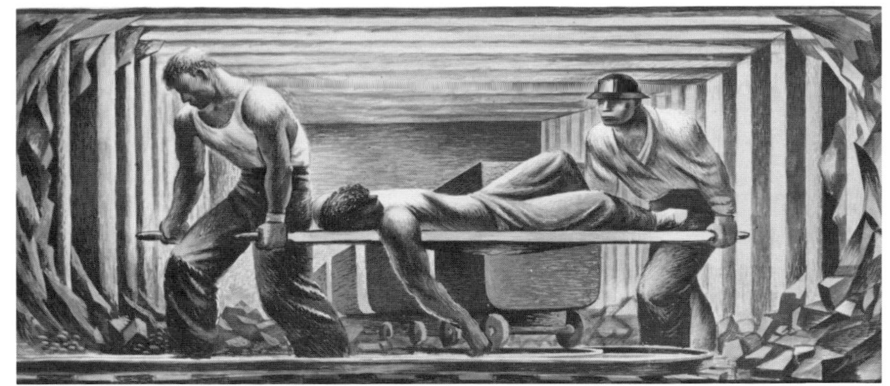

FLETCHER MARTIN
MINE RESCUE
1939
TEMPERA ON PANEL
15 x 36"
COLLECTION NATIONAL MUSEUM OF AMERICAN ART
SMITHSONIAN INSTITUTION
COURTESY UNIVERSITY OF MARYLAND COLLEGE PARK

During his boyhood, Fletcher Martin lived in Emmett, Idaho, where he learned the printing trade from his father, the proprietor of the local newspaper. At sixteen, Martin left home, and after a stint in the merchant marine and the navy, he attended Stickney School of Art in Los Angeles. There, he took the opportunity to work in a cooperative art class with David Olfaro Siqueiros, the highly acclaimed Mexican muralist. Impressed by Siqueiros' spirited ideas and bold painting techniques, Martin briefly assisted Siqueiros on a project and later embarked on his own successful career as a muralist.

In the 1930s, The Federal Art Project, a branch of the Works Projects Administration, employed thousands of artists throughout the country to decorate public buildings with works of art. One specific program was the "48 States Competition," a contest devised to place a mural in a public post office in each state. Of the 1,477 proposals submitted, none was more controversial than Fletcher Martin's winning design for the Kellogg, Idaho, post office.

For the competition, Martin chose to illustrate a theme that was sympathetic to the plight of mine workers exposed to hazardous conditions. Entitled *Mine Rescue*, his mural entry depicts two husky miners carrying an injured worker on a stretcher from a mineshaft. The painting brought immediate criticism from the local mining industry as well as from the state art association for its suggestion of disaster. "The intimate connection between home, work, and communal identity accounts for the bitter dispute that erupted in Kellogg, Idaho, in 1939 when an artist submitted a mural design showing a fatal accident in a local lead mine. The pictorial equation of work with catastrophe was intolerable to the public."[1]

Even though Martin's mural design was a finalist in the 48 States Competition, he was forced to replace it under pressure from the north Idaho community. Martin installed a new mural describing a more palatable historical subject, the discovery of the Bunker Hill and Sullivan mine in 1886 by Noah Kellogg, Phil O'Rourke, and their burro. Martin's second mural, although not nearly as artistically strong as the original, did, however, appease public outcry.

Born April 29, 1904, in Palisades, Colorado. Graduate of Clarkston, Washington, high school. Served in U.S. Navy, 1922-26. Studied art, exhibited, and taught in Los Angeles. Designed WPA post office murals for San Pedro, California; Lamesa, Texas: and Kellogg, Idaho. Prepared mural proposal for Ada County courthouse, 1930. Head of Dept. of Painting and Drawing, Kansas City Art Institute, 1940s. Artist-correspondent for Life, *W.W. II. Taught at Art Students League, Univ. of Iowa, other institutions. Published illustrations; exhibited at 1939 New York World's Fair and 1940 Golden Gate International Exposition. Work in Denver Art Museum, de Young Museum, Los Angeles County Museum, Museum of Modern Art. Living in Guanajuato, Mexico, in 1976.*

1. Marling, Karal Ann. *Wall-to-Wall America* (Minneapolis: University of Minnesota Press, 1982) 19.

HARRY PARNELL

Harry Parnell was a political cartoonist for the *Idaho Daily Statesman* who, for unknown reasons, came to the Horseshoe Bend area of Idaho about 1944. He was a squatter who supposedly liked the roar of the river so much that he built a house of stone three miles north of town on the banks of the Payette. It was an ingenious structure in which a water-wheel provided power and a rock outcropping in the floor of the house functioned as a built-in cookstove. Parnell, who was looked upon as an eccentric, lived on the river for over twenty-five years.

The expressive portrait of Irishman John Hogan was painted by Parnell in 1948, long after Hogan's death. He holds a place in early Boise history as an obscure figure known locally as "Hogan the Stiff," because his misadventures, often timed to secure winter quarters, made him a regular boarder at the city jail. The painting, composed in boldly outlined forms, was copied from an old photograph and portrays this mischievous character, not as a vagrant or criminal, but as an Irish immigrant in his Sunday best suit. Perhaps Parnell's own eccentric nature made him sympathetic to Hogan's misguided life.

HARRY PARNELL
JAMES HOGAN
1948
OIL ON BOARD
11¼ × 9″
COLLECTION IDAHO STATE HISTORICAL SOCIETY

ROBERT WILLIAM ADDISON

Born January 17, 1924, in Boise, Idaho. Studied at Boise Junior College after W.W. II. B.A., School of the Art Institute of Chicago. Self-taught commercial artist; began exhibiting fine art in the mid-1950s. Resided in Chicago until his death, April 14, 1988. Has exhibited at Riverside Galleries and R. W. Norton Gallery in Shreveport, La.; Idaho State Exhibition; Mississippi Valley Artists Exhibition, Springfield, Ill.; and in Chicago at Merrill Chase Galleries, Gilman Galleries, Standard Club Art Show, Navy Pier Show, Union League Club of Chicago. Subject of a retrospective exhibition in 1971 at R. W. Norton and a 40-year retrospective at Merrill Chase Galleries in 1982. Work in the permanent collection of the Illinois State Museum, Springfield, and the Art Institute of Chicago.

As a young boy in the 1930s, Robert Addison first saw the works of twentieth-century artists at the newly constructed Boise Gallery of Art. Here, in the original sandstone Gallery built under the Works Progress Administration, he viewed works by Edward Hopper, Peter Hurd, Grant Wood, and artists of the Ashcan school. Addison related that this experience "is probably what inspired me to take art seriously."[1]

Addison, who throughout his life was intrigued by art and architecture, first aspired to become an architect, but his plans were interrupted by World War II. Just out of high school at the time of war, he enlisted in the service, but was injured in basic training. During convalescence, a Red Cross therapist encouraged him to paint with watercolors and arranged for his first one-man show. Encouraged by this initial success, he enrolled through the G.I. Bill at the Art Institute of Chicago. While in school Addison made a practical decision to become a commercial artist. During the day he studied fine arts and at night taught himself advertising layout and design. Following graduation, he joined a Chicago firm where assignments included magazine illustrations, covers for the *Saturday Evening Post*, and advertisements for *Collier's* and *Time*.

Foreshadowing his later style, Addison's early works contain characteristic elements seen throughout his career: architectural forms, value contrasts, the illusion of space, dynamic angles, and rhythmic patterns. In his 1949 *View of Boise*, the atmospheric mood is charged with drama and the depth of space is intensified by streams of light, an effect which is a distinguishing feature of Addison's style. He explained, "Everything we see is based on light. It makes our eyes work and it determines where we are and our dimensions."[2]

1. Thornton, Alix. "Close-Up: Robert W. Addison." *Avenue* M April 1987: 21.
2. Thornton.

ROBERT W. ADDISON
VIEW OF BOISE
1949
OIL ON CANVAS
25⅛ × 29¾"
COLLECTION MRS. ROBERT W. ADDISON

MARY KIRKWOOD

MARY KIRKWOOD
WHEAT STUBBLE
1948
OIL ON CANVAS
23¾ x 33"
COLLECTION UNIVERSITY OF IDAHO
LIONEL HAMPTON SCHOOL OF MUSIC

Born December 21, 1904, in Hillsboro, Oregon. Grew up in Missoula, Montana. B.A., University of Montana, 1926; M.F.A. University of Oregon, 1930. Additional study at Harvard University in summers of 1932-33; at the Royal Art School in Stockholm, Sweden, 1933-34; and under Joseph Stefanelli and Robert Goldwater in Paris, 1967. Came to University of Idaho in 1930; taught design, composition, art history, and life drawing. Taught eight summers with U. of I. Workshops on Wheels in Coeur d'Alene, Stanley and McCall. Began the Idaho Art Association. Numerous one-person exhibitions in Oregon, eastern Washington, and Idaho, including a retrospective in 1982 at the University Gallery, Moscow; participated in group exhibitions since the 1930s, particularly in Western States. Work in Cheney Cowles Museum, Boise Art Museum, University of Idaho, corporate collection of IBM, Bank of Idaho, and Boise Cascade, and many private collections. Retired as professor of art in 1970 and resides in Moscow.

The 1920s and '30s, when Mary Kirkwood studied painting, were a swiftly changing time in which abstraction emerged as the dominant style on the American art scene. While the leading artists of the day exchanged representational subjects for modes of abstraction, Mary Kirkwood maintained a steadfast interest in portraying the human figure.

A native of the Northwest, Kirkwood was born in 1904 in Oregon, but spent her formative years in Montana. Her studies at the University of Montana and later at the University of Oregon, where she earned her Master of Fine Arts degree, provided her with a formal academic background, especially in the knowledge of figure painting. "As a young student, creativity implied abstraction. Yet I loved the human qualities of the subject above all, and any abstraction which used the figure merely as another object in the painting or just an element in design seemed to dehumanize it, making this path impossible to me."[1]

Kirkwood sought to resolve her dilemma of how to express realist forms within the context of abstraction. She traveled east to attend art school, first at Harvard and then in Europe at the Royal Art School in Stockholm, Sweden. These experiences were paramount in broadening her artistic outlook. In Sweden, under Otto Skold, Kirkwood translated her literal realist techniques into a more fluid method of painting which relied upon expression without the conscious awareness of brush technique. She discovered that abstraction was not purely invention, but could consist of shapes inherent in the forms themselves.

MARY KIRKWOOD
KATHRYN KENNARD VAUGHT
1948
OIL ON CANVAS
48 × 38"
COLLECTION UNIVERSITY OF IDAHO
LIONEL HAMPTON SCHOOL OF MUSIC

On her return to the Northwest, Kirkwood was encouraged to join the faculty at the University of Idaho by Ted Prichard, the founder of the Department of Art and Architecture. Kirkwood's energy for teaching went hand in hand with her verve for painting. For more than forty years Mary Kirkwood influenced, guided, and encouraged art students at the University. A giving person, she found educating as fulfilling as the rewards of painting. Over the decades, scores of art students at the University of Idaho have listened to Kirkwood's sensitive advice and gained from her instruction.

1. *Mary Kirkwood Retrospective Exhibition* (Moscow: University of Idaho Gallery, 1982) 2.

ARCHIE BOYD TEATER

Archie Teater spent much of his youth in the Hagerman Valley, where he was motivated to paint by his love of the ruggedly beautiful and richly varied landscape. During the Depression years, he pursued his artistic career by journeying through the mountains to paint mining and lumber camps in Boise Basin. Leading a vagabond life, he painted camp scenes and occasionally panned for gold along the Snake River. Early on, he made regular painting excursions to the Tetons. In Jackson Hole, he met his future wife, Patricia, who became his strongest supporter and encouraged him to attend the Art Students League in New York City.

Though based in Hagerman, the Teaters were not full-time residents of the valley. Most years they stayed only two months in the spring and two in the fall, spending summers in a log studio in Wyoming. They toured the world during the interim, roving through Europe, South America, Australia; over the years they traveled to more than one hundred countries.

An extremely prolific artist, Teater produced hundreds of landscapes, portraits, and still lifes. His subject matter ranges from scenes of southern Idaho to picturesque landscapes in exotic foreign places. Whatever he saw became a subject for his brush. In

Born in Boise, Idaho, May 5, 1901. Studied at the Portland Art Museum in Oregon, the Art Students League, New York, and in Europe and Asia. Participated in Idaho Public Works of Art Program, 1930s. Married Patricia A. Wilson, 1941. Worked as free-lance painter maintaining studios in Jackson Hole, Wyoming, and at Bliss, Idaho. Awards from American Artists' Professional League, 1957, for landscape painting; silver seal of the State of Idaho, 1971; Boise State University's medallion for distinguished service, 1971; Idaho Statesman's Distinguished Citizen award, 1971. Exhibited with the Boise Art Association and throughout the country; represented in many private and public collections. Died July 19, 1978.

ARCHIE BOYD TEATER
TEATER STUDIO GARDEN
CIRCA 1950s
OIL ON CANVAS
26 × 40"
COLLECTION LARRY MEIEROTTO AND MARY ABERCROMBIE
COURTESY YATES-FRITCHMAN GALLERIES

his early years, winter found him heading out in snowshoes to capture remote spots in the Sawtooth Mountains. In summer, he depicted the Teton Range and the cattle, cowboys, and sagebrush-covered hills of Idaho. He once remarked that he had "painted the Snake River from its headwaters until it joins the Columbia."[1]

In 1951, the Teaters conceived the idea of building a studio on the cliff rim of the Snake River Canyon above Hagerman. Through a mutual acquaintance, they contacted Frank Lloyd Wright and commissioned him to design a 2,000-square-foot studio, significant today as one of two Wright structures in Idaho. The house was constructed at a spectacular site on a rocky cliff overlooking the raging rapids of the Snake River. The building is an excellent example of what Wright called "organic architecture," in which harmony is maintained between building and site. This rock and glass studio served as inspiration for Teater, who referred to it as his "fountainhead or creative wellspring."[2] *Teater Studio Garden* was painted from its front window and shows the lava rock knoll with a path meandering across the property and a view of distant mountains. For seventy years, Teater divided his time between home and traveling; he found creative energy in Hagerman Valley while his nomadic way of life led him to visit the remotest regions of the world.

1. Turner, Faith. "Boisean Winning Fame as Artist." *Idaho Daily Statesman* 10 Dec. 1939.
2. Turner

ARCHIE BOYD TEATER
PINK LILY POND
CIRCA 1950s
OIL ON CANVAS
30 × 50"
COLLECTION LARRY MEIEROTTO AND MARY ABERCROMBIE
COURTESY YATES-FRITCHMAN GALLERIES

DON BEMCO BENNETT

DON BEMCO BENNETT
HELL ROARING LAKE
CIRCA 1950s
ACRYLIC ON PANEL
30 × 40"
COLLECTION DON BEMCO BENNETT

Born January 8, 1916, in McGlaughlin, South Dakota. Educated at Lewis and Clark High School, Spokane; B.F.A., University of Washington; Edison Vocational School, Seattle; further study in Seattle and California, including watercolor technique with Eliot O'Hara. Has lived in Ketchum since the early 1950s, specializing in landscape and natural subjects. Has exhibited widely across the U.S. and abroad, including Corcoran Gallery, 1946; U.S.I.A. Worldwide Traveling Exhibit, 1960; Springfield, Mass., 1964; Fry Museum, Seattle, 1968; University of Minnesota, 1971. Recipient of various awards. Wrote and illustrated for Ford Times, *published landscapes in "Treasures of Western Art" print series. Works owned by Cheney Cowles Museum, Ford Motor Co. Collection, Boise Cascade Corp., ITT Sheraton Corp., other institutions and many private collectors. Currently lives with his wife, Doris, in Ketchum, Idaho.*

Mountaineer, skier, and painter, Don Bennett is fortunate to have successfully combined two lifelong passions — the love of nature and the outdoors, and his talent for art. His fascination with nature began as he was growing up at Bonners Ferry in northern Idaho and in the Cascades region of Washington. For Bennett, the sight of majestic mountains and crystalline streams has been a continuous source of inspiration.

As a student in Seattle, Bennett pursued a fine arts degree at the University of Washington, followed by several years working in commercial art and in mountain reconnaissance for the army. During World War II, he sailed with the merchant marine, but never ceased to paint. During his tour of duty, brushes and watercolor paper went into a seabag instead of the usual mountain rucksack. He took every opportunity to paint in remote corners of the world, and by the war's end he had accumulated a portfolio of sketches and watercolors portraying Australia, Ceylon, India, and Africa. Returning to Seattle after the war, he again worked in the commercial art field, but the allure of the Idaho mountains beckoned; Bennett and his family left the tensions of city life to settle in Sun Valley.

Bennett is a purist who depicts only the places he has experienced and never paints from slides or photographs. Painting out-of-doors is demanding, requiring exceptional patience and also special equipment, which the artist has designed himself. One invention was a portable easel mounted on ski poles for painting winter scenes, while another was an artist's survival kit with drawing materials in a small, easily carried container. Bennett admits the difficulty of contending with the weather, the insects, and other burdens of open air work, but feels it is an important discipline for a landscape painter. Although Bennett paints in a variety of mediums, he is most prolific in watercolors. "You don't want to be stuck up in the boondocks with wet oils," he says. Bennett labels himself half-artist, half-naturalist, and continues to paint and live in Ketchum, Idaho, amid the spectacular beauty of the Sawtooths.

THOMAS RAYMOND NEILSON

THOMAS RAYMOND NEILSON
WINTER ON PORTNEUF
CIRCA 1940
OIL ON CANVAS
15 × 20"
IDAHO STATE UNIVERSITY
STUDENT UNION PERMANENT ART COLLECTION

During the 1920s and '30s T. R. Neilson became known throughout southern Idaho as an outstanding promoter of the arts. He began his career as supervisor of music and art in the Payette and Fruitland schools. He went on to teach music in the Nampa and Caldwell public schools for several years before moving across the state to Pocatello. With an admirable teaching record to his credit, he was appointed Director of Music and Fine Arts at the Idaho Technical Institute, which has since become Idaho State University. Neilson made significant strides toward advancing arts education in the Pacific Northwest. Among his most noteworthy contributions is his series of eighteen art instructional handbooks for children, which achieved a circulation of 500,000 copies. A community-minded person, Neilson donated paintings from his personal collection to the University, providing the nucleus for what became the Neilson Art Gallery, now enlarged and known as Transition Gallery at Idaho State University.

Aside from being a teacher and supporter of the arts, Neilson was also a prolific painter whose landscapes depict many southern Idaho locations. In his snow scene on the banks of the Portneuf, Neilson mirrors a cold evening during the dark months of midwinter. His painting style is impressionistic, a technical approach most likely influenced by his early art classes at the Metropolitan Museum of Art School and the Art Students League in New York. Nielson's multiple gifts to Idaho, both as a painter of hearty landscapes and as an influential educator, are deservedly remembered and appreciated.

Born in Sunbury, Ohio, on April 26, 1880. Educated at Ohio Wesleyan University, Delaware, Ohio; American Conservatory; Augsburg Art School; Art Students League. Studied portraiture at Metropolitan Art School, New York, and under A. K. Cross, Maine Art School. Came to Idaho in 1910. Worked 10 years as supervisor of music and art in southwest Idaho public schools. Director of Schools of Music and Fine Arts at Idaho State University, Pocatello, 1921; head of art department, 1929 to 1947. Began annual Pocatello art shows, 1935. Exhibited at Salt Lake City and Springville, Utah, Heyburn, and Boise as well as Seattle, Spokane, Portland, and cities in the Midwest and East. Named Professor Emeritus at retirement, as was his wife, Professor of Music Mayme Ingard Neilson. Moved in 1950 to Los Altos, California, where he died January 19, 1959.

OLIVER PARSON

In an earthy realist manner, artist and educator Oliver Parson describes the West of a vanished time. Living in Utah and eastern Idaho for thirty-five years, he explored and painted the back reaches of the intermountain region. In oil and watercolors, he visually captures its hidden places and its people with insight and a touch of romance.

Parson taught art at a junior high school in Salt Lake City as well as both junior and senior high school in Springville, Utah. He also found time during his busy teaching career to serve as curator of the Springville Art Gallery. During the 1950s he moved to Rexburg, Idaho, to became head of the Art Department at Ricks College, where he taught for nineteen years.

He paints in a "semi-impressionist" style and says of his work, "I paint direct, while on the spot. I try to use the things of nature, taking liberties, to create the mood felt at the place. I especially work for a brilliant contrast of light and shadow."[1] Adept at watercolors as well as oils, he counts among his favorite subjects mountain scenes and old abandoned buildings.

In *Old Merrit Ranch*, Parson describes with thick swathing brush strokes several ramshackle cabins with swagging roofs. Like many of his paintings, this work has a story. Just off a dirt road high in the Sawtooths, the remains of a few cabins known as the old Merrit ranch are nestled in the trees. The cluster of cabins, long deserted, has gained a reputation as a ghost ranch. Rumored to be a distillery during the 1920s, the place is said to have been the stronghold of moonshiners.

As viewed during the 1950s, set among the tall pines, the ranch is seen with foundations askew, roofs sagging, planks sticking up, and panes gone from the windows. Some cabins still contained dilapidated wood-burning stoves such as the one pictured outside the cabin on the right. Covering the floor of the cabin on the left were hundreds of gallon jugs, recalling the long gone days of Prohibition.

Oliver Parson now lives in California, and is warmly remembered for his professional years of instructing Idaho's youth and his romantic interpretations of the rustic beauty of Idaho.

1. Junior League of Boise. *Library of Originals: Idaho Artists Exhibit*, 1958.

Born in Kansas in 1916. B.S., 1941, and M.F.A., 1948, from University of Utah. Further study at University of Southern California, University of Colorado, Brigham Young University, Colorado State University, National Academy of Fine Arts, Art Students League. Taught junior and senior high school in Utah. Curator of the Springville Art Museum in Utah, 1947-1954. Appointed professor of art in 1954 at Ricks College, Rexburg, Idaho; became head of the art department and remained at Ricks until 1973. President of Utah and Idaho Art Associations; member of Idaho Commission of Arts and Humanities; recipient of 4th Biennial Governor's Award in the Arts, 1976. Exhibited one-man shows in Idaho, Utah and other western states, and in the de Young Museum, San Francisco. Now living in Placentia, California.

OLIVER PARSON
OLD MERRIT RANCH
1958
OIL ON MASONITE
23½ × 35½"
COLLECTION BOISE ART MUSEUM

ALFRED DUNN

Born November 22, 1909, in Los Angeles, California. Raised in Twin Falls, Idaho. B.A., 1936, University of Idaho; M.F.A., California College of Arts and Crafts, Oakland. Worked five years as art director for Acme Press of Seattle. Participated in Idaho Public Works of Art Project, 1930s. Professor of art, University of Idaho, 1941 to 1974. Exhibited in Federation of Rocky Mountain States shows, Idaho exhibitions, Ford Motor Co. and U.S.I.A. traveling shows abroad. Published illustrations in books and magazines, including Ford Times; *designed and illustrated* Beacon for Mountain and Plain *by Rafe Gibbs and many University of Idaho publications. Recipient of various watercolor awards. Works in Latah County Historical Society, Boise Art Museum, and many public and private collections. Resides in Moscow, Idaho.*

For nearly fifty years, the scenic Idaho landscape of wide open spaces and rural communities inspired Alf Dunn to paint. In carefully detailed watercolors, he has reflected the character of small town life and conveyed the changing mood and variety of the state's terrain with sensitivity and insight. An Idaho resident for most of his lifetime, Dunn was raised in Twin Falls, graduated from the University of Idaho in 1936, and for several years attended the California College of Arts and Crafts, where he earned a Master of Fine Arts degree. He then worked as a commercial artist for five years in Seattle before coming to teach at the University of Idaho in 1941. A faculty member for thirty-three years, he focused on design and watercolor classes during his career.

In addition to teaching, Alf Dunn for many years designed artwork for University of Idaho publications, contributed drawings to magazine articles and illustrated books. Watercolor is his medium of choice because he feels it is ideally suited to the soft colors and rolling hills of northern Idaho. In hundreds of watercolors produced during his residence in Moscow, Dunn recorded not only the surrounding countryside, but most of the interesting structures of the town. Railroad yards, university buildings, and local industry all are among his chosen subjects. Moscow, aside from being a university town, is also known for its agricultural and clay products industry. In *Brick Plant on 8th Street, Moscow,* Dunn depicts the firing kilns used in clay processing. His quick fluid brush strokes give the scene a sense of immediacy. Alf Dunn, now retired from teaching, continues to live and work in Moscow, Idaho.

ALF DUNN
BRICK PLANT, 8TH STREET, MOSCOW
1943
WATERCOLOR ON PAPER
13⅞ × 19⅛"
COLLECTION LATAH COUNTY HISTORICAL SOCIETY

ARNOLD WESTERLUND

ARNOLD WESTERLUND
CARAVELLE — SHIPS IN THE NIGHT
CIRCA 1950s
ETCHING WITH FOUND FORMS
13½ × 12½"
COLLECTION MARCIA ANDERSON
COURTESY OF THE ARTIST

Born September 10, 1914, in Bemidji, Minnesota. Graduate of Coeur d'Alene High School. B.A., 1938 and M.A., 1939, University of Idaho. Further study at Columbia University, University of Oregon, Washington State College and University of Washington. Taught art and music in Gooding Public Schools, 1939-41; taught in Clarkston, Washington, Public Schools, 1941-49. Taught summer classes at the College of Idaho and Albion State College. Professor of art, University of Idaho, 1949-1976. Exhibited in National Collagraphic Print Show, Krannert Museum of University of Illinois, Northwest Printmaker's Show in Seattle, university and private galleries in the Northwest, Boise Gallery of Art. Has traveled widely in Europe, Central America, and Japan. Resides in Moscow, Idaho.

The art of printmaking has engaged the interest of accomplished artist Arnold Westerlund throughout his career. His particular passion has been collagraphy, an offshoot of the etching process in which images are derived from the imprint of found objects. Westerlund's early printmaking experiments using additive materials led him to study the techniques of Glen Alps, University of Washington professor and inventor of this unique printing process.

The major difference between collagraphy and other printmaking techniques is that the surface of the printing plate is built up rather than incised, as in etching or engraving. A collagraph is created when a collage of objects is adhered to a plate, rubbed with ink, and passed through a press to form an image on paper. In *Caravelle*, one of his early works, Westerlund used aluminum foil, sandpaper, and shells as sources of shapes and textures. Sometimes he incorporated household spices, seeds, and herbs to add surface interest. Today the artist favors industrial materials, such as TV and radio components and automotive parts. Westerlund finds that gears and gaskets, when printed, are reminiscent of futuristic or interstellar objects. Recognized as a pioneer of this printing process, Westerlund was included in the first national collagraph show held at Pratt Institute in New York in 1976.

Arnold Westerlund has combined his talents as an artist with dedication to the teaching profession. For ten years he taught art and music at elementary and secondary schools in Idaho and Washington, before coming to the University of Idaho to teach art classes and printmaking. Now retired after a twenty-eight year career at the University, Westerlund remains devoted to his art and continues to experiment with different techniques to refine his artistry.

GEORGE ROBERTS

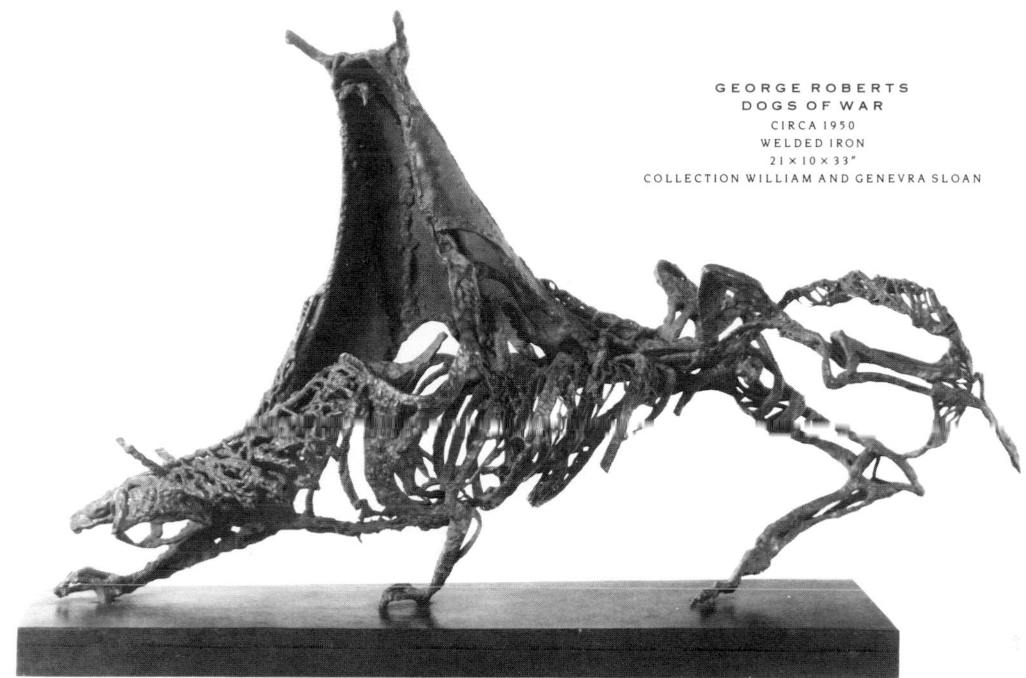

GEORGE ROBERTS
DOGS OF WAR
CIRCA 1950
WELDED IRON
21 × 10 × 33"
COLLECTION WILLIAM AND GENEVRA SLOAN

Feisty and affable, George Roberts is recognized as a driving force of the art department at the University of Idaho in Moscow. A professor for thirty years and chairman of the department for fourteen, Roberts says that during his tenure he "taught every aspect of art except lithography and weaving." A self-proclaimed artistic "jack-of-all-trades," Roberts participated in a spectrum of activities from lecturing and giving instruction to jurying exhibits and installing shows. A highly respected artist, Roberts is best known for his large-scale sculptures primarily produced in cold-rolled steel and iron.

For Roberts, the material and the process of making sculpture hold special significance. Since he began sculpting, his iron work has been based on line drawings with brush and ink. "Translating the drawing to a three-dimensional form is like drawing in space. It's like having great strength; you can model steel with your fingertips almost like clay. Negative space becomes very important, inside, out and around."[1] Roberts sees sculpting in iron as a direct art form involving little metamorphosis, unlike sculptural mediums such as bronze casting or ceramics.

George Roberts' iron sculpture *Dogs of War* suggests opposing forms writhing in conflict. The piece was inspired by Mark Antony's speech in *Julius Caesar* in which he prophesies "fierce civil strife...blood and destruction" as the aftermath of Caesar's murder. During the 1950s several young architects from Spokane proposed that *Dogs of War* be produced in a twelve-foot-high version as an indictment of war, erected in memory of World War II. The final project, however, was dismissed and the large-scale work was never completed. Like the conflicting forces of this sculpture, George Roberts seeks to balance two extremes in his art: the eloquence of flowing line with the vigor of hard steel.

1. George Roberts, letter to Boise Art Museum, 18 Feb. 1990.

Born June 10, 1927, in Madison, Wisconsin. B.S. and M.S., University of Wisconsin; studied ceramics with Harvey Littleton and Toshiko Takaezu and sculpture with Humberto Albrizio and Lou Weinberg. Served in U.S. Merchant Marine 1947-49. Came to University of Idaho, 1957; chairman of the art department 1963-1977. Taught summers in New Mexico, Washington, British Columbia, and Alaska as well as with Idaho Workshop on Wheels. Recipient of Outstanding Teaching Award; Idaho Governor's Award and Medal for Excellence in the Arts, 1981. Created numerous works for University of Idaho, and public and private commissions. Exhibited extensively throughout the United States, in many ceramics and crafts invitational exhibitions in western states and Japan; Seattle World's Fair, 1963, and Spokane Exposition, 1974; University of Wisconsin 50 Year Alumni Exhibition, 1980; Idaho Artists Biennial exhibitions since the 1950s. Currently professor of art and acting associate dean at the University of Idaho.

PATRICK FLAMMIA

Patrick Flammia, son of an Italian family that settled on the East Coast, was raised near Boston, Massachusetts. During World War II, he served as a sergeant in the Army Tank Corps in Europe. When he returned to the United States after the war, he attended art classes at the Art Students League in New York, the Ringling School of Art in Sarasota, Florida, and later the prestigious Rhode Island School of Design. Upon completion of his studies, he moved west to Coeur d'Alene, Idaho, joining his father-in-law in the lumber business. Flammia's oil canvas *Log Jammer*, executed about the time he moved to Idaho, depicts equipment used in harvesting timber. The canvas sings with motion and color. Flammia's painting style here shows evidence of his New York training during the 1940s, when abstraction was in the forefront of art theory.

Patrick Flammia has maintained an active involvement in the arts since coming to Idaho. He initially worked with Harold Balazs, a Spokane sculptor, on a joint ironwork project. An art instructor for many years, Flammia taught at elementary and secondary schools as well as at North Idaho College. He has also conducted life-drawing classes at his home in Coeur d'Alene for more than fifteen years. More recently, he and his wife, Sue Flammia, have been deeply involved in supporting the community's flourishing Art on the Green Festival, an outstanding annual summer event which they helped establish in 1968. Recipients of the 1987 Patrons of the Arts Award from the Coeur d'Alene Peforming Arts Alliance, the Flammias were further honored in 1990 with the Governor's Award for Support in the Arts.

Born February 15, 1923, in Boston, Massachusetts. Studied art between 1940 and 1950 at Ringling School of Art and Amagansett School of Art, Sarasota, Florida; Art Students League; Rhode Island School of Design. Served in W.W. II, 1942-45. Moved to Idaho, 1950. Awarded first place in 1950 Rhode Island Annual and 7th Pacific Northwest Annual. Has exhibited at Cheney Cowles Museum, Northwest area college and university galleries, and private galleries in Coeur d'Alene, Sandpoint, and Spokane. Works in North Idaho corporate collections and many private collections in the United States and abroad. Currently lives with his wife Sue on Lake Coeur d'Alene.

PATRICK FLAMMIA
LOG JAMMER
1950
OIL ON CANVAS BOARD
$11\frac{7}{8} \times 15\frac{1}{2}$"
COLLECTION CHENEY COWLES MUSEUM

CONAN MATHEWS

Born September 16, 1905, in Providence, Utah. B.A., *College of Idaho, 1936;* M.F.A., *University of Utah, 1951. Further study at Utah State, California School of Fine Arts, University of California, University of Denver, Columbia University. Taught two years at California School of Fine Arts; three at College of Idaho. Head of art department, Boise Junior College, 1939-41; acting president of the College, 1941-45; dean of faculty 1946-56. President of Boise Art Association, 1945-50. Published Sunday art column for* Idaho Statesman *for eight years. Joined Brigham Young University art faculty, 1956; department chairman and dean of College of Fine Arts and Communications, 1959-1967. Died October 30, 1972. Exhibited at New York World's Fair, 1939; painted Idaho exhibit murals for San Francisco World's Fair, 1940. One-man exhibits in 1937 and 1938 at Boise Art Gallery; others at San Francisco and Santa Rosa, California, Coeur d'Alene, Seattle, Salt Lake City and Logan.*

At the time of World War II, Conan Mathews was an influential Idaho art instructor who promoted abstraction and encouraged his students to develop modernist attitudes. Mathews was a professor of art for three years at College of Idaho and for seventeen years at Boise Junior College, where he became academic dean. A progressive teacher and writer, he was involved in many cultural activities and contributed frequently to journals on art and education. Widely praised for his leadership, Mathews continued his career at Brigham Young University, where he was instrumental in creating the Harris Fine Arts Center. In addition to being a prominent educator, Mathews was a highly regarded artist who exhibited oil paintings and watercolors throughout the West.

Mathews' broad education included study at California School of Fine Arts in San Francisco and at the University of Utah, where he worked under well-known landscape artist Birger Sandzen. He undertook post-graduate study with the important European abstractionist Hans Hofmann of Munich, Germany. In Mathews' painting entitled *Landscape*, one can see Hofmann's influence in the abstract composition. Of his own work Mathews states: "It is inevitable that the artist distort in his work. The modern artist realizes that he cannot improve on nature; he cannot even copy it and do it justice so he doesn't try. Nature is his inspiration and point of departure."[1] Through his writings and art programs, Conan Mathews taught a modern approach and introduced international art concepts to regional students.

1. *Salt Lake Tribune* 24 Sept. 1930.

CONAN MATHEWS
LANDSCAPE
1948
OIL ON MASONITE
27¼ × 23½"
COLLECTION CHENEY COWLES MUSEUM

EXHIBITION CHECKLIST

ARTIST UNKNOWN
CHIEF LAWYER, NEZ PERCE
CIRCA 1900
OIL ON CANVAS
18¾ × 13" OVAL
COLLECTION NEZ PERCE
NATIONAL HISTORICAL PARK
NATIONAL PARK SERVICE

ARTIST UNKNOWN
DIANA THE HUNTRESS
CIRCA 1890
OIL ON CANVAS
56 × 36"
COLLECTION IDAHO CITY HISTORICAL FOUNDATION, INC.

ARTIST UNKNOWN
GOLD MINER
CIRCA 1940
OIL ON BOARD
15⅞ × 19¾"
COLLECTION IDAHO CITY HISTORICAL FOUNDATION, INC.

ARTIST UNKNOWN
MOSCOW, IDAHO
HISTORY OF THE PACIFIC NORTHWEST: OREGON AND WASHINGTON,
BY ELWOOD EVANS
1889
LITHOGRAPH
6 11/16 × 9¼"
COURTESY CAROLYN STALEY FINE PRINTS
SEATTLE, WASHINGTON

ARTIST UNKNOWN
ROSSI LOGGING CAMP, PHEIFFER CREEK
1902
WATERCOLOR AND GOUACHE ON PAPER
17⅞ × 30"
COLLECTION IDAHO CITY HISTORICAL FOUNDATION, INC.

ARTIST UNKNOWN
VICTORIAN LADY
CIRCA 1900
OIL ON CANVAS
22 × 16¾"
PRIVATE COLLECTION

ROBERT W. ADDISON
VIEW OF BOISE
1949
OIL ON CANVAS
25⅛ × 29¾"
COLLECTION MRS. ROBERT W. ADDISON

ROWENA CLEMENT LUNG ALCORN
SPALDING MISSION CABIN
1936
OIL ON CANVAS
17½ × 23½"
COLLECTION NEZ PERCE
NATIONAL HISTORICAL PARK
NATIONAL PARK SERVICE

PORTRAIT OF HENRY HARMON SPALDING
1936
OIL ON CANVAS
31⅝ × 23⅜"
COLLECTION NEZ PERCE
NATIONAL HISTORICAL PARK
NATIONAL PARK SERVICE

JAMES MADISON ALDEN
SINYAKWATEEN DEPOT FROM NEAR LEFT BANK OF CLARKE'S FORK LOOKING UP
CIRCA 1860
WATERCOLOR ON PAPER
9¾ × 13⅛"
COLLECTION NATIONAL ARCHIVES
WASHINGTON, D.C.

VIEW FROM SUMMIT OF ''LOOKOUT MOUNTAIN,'' RIGHT BANK OF CLARKE'S FORK OPPOSITE SINYAKWATEEN, SHOWING KELLISPELM OR PEND'OREILLE LAKE IN THE DISTANCE
CIRCA 1860
WATERCOLOR ON PAPER
10 × 13¾"
COLLECTION NATIONAL ARCHIVES
WASHINGTON, D.C.

KELLISPELM LAKE OR PEND'OREILLE LAKE, FROM ''VIEW POINT'' NEAR WHERE CLARKE'S FORK FLOWS FROM THE LAKE
CIRCA 1860
WATERCOLOR ON PAPER
9⅞ × 13¼"
COLLECTION NATIONAL ARCHIVES
WASHINGTON, D.C.

HELEN HOFF AUPPERLE
''RUNNING BEAR''—WILLIE GEORGE
CIRCA 1940
OIL ON CANVAS
48 × 36"
COLLECTION DON AUPPERLE

SAWTOOTHS SUNSET
CIRCA 1950s
WATERCOLOR ON PAPER
20 × 25"
COLLECTION BOISE ART MUSEUM

T. N. BARNARD AND NELLIE STOCKBRIDGE
PLACER MINING, DELTA
N.D.
SEPIA TONED PRINT
11 × 14"
COURTESY UNIVERSITY OF IDAHO LIBRARY

ROTARY SNOWPLOW ON THE S-BRIDGE
N.D.
SEPIA TONED PRINT
11 × 14"
COURTESY UNIVERSITY OF IDAHO LIBRARY

PICNIC PARTY IN BOATS
1897
SEPIA TONED PRINT
11 × 14"
COURTESY UNIVERSITY OF IDAHO LIBRARY

DON BEMCO BENNETT
HELL ROARING LAKE
CIRCA 1950s
ACRYLIC ON PANEL
30 × 40"
COLLECTION DON BEMCO BENNETT

KANE CANYON
CIRCA 1950s
OIL ON PANEL
24 × 30"
COLLECTION DON BEMCO BENNETT

CLIFFORD K. BERRYMAN
MODERNIST BORAH PAINTS AN ''OLD MASTER!''
1920s-1930s
INK ON PAPER
13 1/8 × 14"
COLLECTION IDAHO STATE HISTORICAL SOCIETY LIBRARY AND ARCHIVES

I DON'T KNOW ANYTHING ABOUT IT
1920s-1930s
INK ON PAPER
13 1/8 × 14"
COLLECTION IDAHO STATE HISTORICAL SOCIETY LIBRARY AND ARCHIVES

AW WOT'S THE USE? THEY BOTH LEAK!
1920s-1930s
INK ON PAPER
13 1/8 × 14"
COLLECTION IDAHO STATE HISTORICAL SOCIETY LIBRARY AND ARCHIVES

MARY ELIZABETH BLACK
PAYNE'S FERRY, IDAHO
1877
OIL ON CANVAS
23 1/2 × 35 1/2"
COLLECTION IDAHO STATE HISTORICAL SOCIETY

SHOSHONE FALLS, IDAHO
N.D.
PENCIL ON PAPER
13 × 17"
COLLECTION IDAHO STATE HISTORICAL SOCIETY

SARA ANNETTE BOWMAN
UNTITLED
CIRCA 1900
OIL ON CANVAS
18 × 18"
COLLECTION LATAH COUNTY HISTORICAL SOCIETY

FLOWERS AND FIELDS AROUND MOSCOW
LEATHER PORTFOLIO WITH WATERCOLOR DRAWINGS
CIRCA 1904
10 × 7 1/2" BINDER
COLLECTION UNIVERSITY OF IDAHO LIBRARY

MRS. M. J. BRADLEY
GEM, IDAHO AND GEM MILL
CIRCA 1890s
OIL ON CANVAS
30 3/4 × 45 7/8"
COLLECTION CHENEY COWLES MUSEUM

BENJAMIN CHAMBERS BROWN
RED FISH LAKE, IDAHO
CIRCA 1900-1940
OIL ON CANVAS
48 × 60"
COLLECTION BOISE PUBLIC LIBRARY

MARGARETTA FAVORITE BROWN
HYDRAULIC MINING IN BOISE BASIN
CIRCA 1870-80
OIL ON CANVAS
26 1/2 × 20 3/4"
COLLECTION IDAHO STATE HISTORICAL SOCIETY

MARGARETTA F. BROWN AND W. M. CAREY
HUNTING DEER IN MOUNTAINS
CIRCA 1880
OIL ON CANVAS
50 × 42"
COLLECTION IDAHO STATE HISTORICAL SOCIETY

ELBRIDGE AYER BURBANK
CHIEF JOSEPH
1898
OIL ON CANVAS
19 × 15"
COURTESY SIDESTREET GALLERY SANDPOINT, IDAHO

CHIEF JOSEPH IN COLVILLE
CIRCA 1902
PENCIL ON PAPER
13 1/2 × 10 1/2"
COURTESY SIDESTREET GALLERY SANDPOINT, IDAHO

FANNY DIKE BURNS
MUSTARD FIELD
1935
OIL ON CANVAS
11 3/4 × 17 1/2"
COLLECTION BOISE ART MUSEUM

LA FAYETTE CARTEE
MAP OF PUBLIC SURVEYS TO ACCOMPANY REPORT TO COMMISSIONER OF THE PUBLIC LAND OFFICE, 1873
AUGUST 20, 1873
INK AND WATERCOLOR ON PAPER
38 1/2 × 28 1/2"
COLLECTION IDAHO STATE HISTORICAL SOCIETY LIBRARY AND ARCHIVES

JAMES CASTLE
TURKEYS
N.D.
COLORED PIGMENT ON CARTON
9 1/2 × 7 5/8"
COLLECTION BOISE ART MUSEM

WOOD STOVE
N.D.
CHARCOAL AND SOOT ON CARDBOARD
8 X 8"
COLLECTION BOISE ART MUSEUM

YARD TOTEMS
N.D.
COLORED PIGMENT AND SOOT ON PAPER
6 15/16 × 10 7/8"
COLLECTION BOISE ART MUSEUM

YARD WITH FANTASY FORMS
N.D.
CHARCOAL, SOOT, WATER ON PAPER
6 3/4 × 8 7/16"
COLLECTION BOISE ART MUSEUM

GEORGE CATLIN
A CROW VILLAGE AND THE SALMON RIVER MOUNTAINS
1855
OIL ON CARDBOARD
15 3/8 × 21 5/8"
COLLECTION NATIONAL GALLERY OF ART, WASHINGTON PAUL MELLON COLLECTION

THREE SHOSHONI WARRIORS ARMED FOR WAR
1855
OIL ON CARDBOARD
15 1/4 × 21 7/8" OVAL
COLLECTION NATIONAL GALLERY OF ART, WASHINGTON PAUL MELLON COLLECTION

IDELLA ROGERS CHESTER
BOISE RIVER BELOW ATLANTA
CIRCA 1909
OIL ON CANVAS
19¾ × 15¾″
COLLECTION MR. AND MRS. JOSEPH A. CHESTER

RUPERTA CHESTER
GREENBACK STAMP MILL, ATLANTA
CIRCA 1909
OIL ON CANVAS
22¾ × 14½″
COLLECTION MR. AND MRS. JOSEPH A. CHESTER

HOT SPRINGS, ATLANTA
CIRCA 1909
OIL ON CANVAS
20 × 13″
COLLECTION MR. AND MRS. JOSEPH A. CHESTER

C. EMMA COLEMAN
VALLEY OF SALUBRIA
CIRCA 1870
OIL ON CANVAS
16⅛ × 13⅛″ OVAL
COLLECTION IDAHO STATE HISTORICAL SOCIETY

HERBERT A. COLLINS
MT. HYNDMAN
1912
OIL ON CANVAS
17½ × 24″
COLLECTION DORAN BUTLER

FISHING ON THE WOOD RIVER
CIRCA 1917-20
OIL ON CANVAS
80 × 71¼″
COLLECTION ROBERT S. MEYER
COURTESY RICHARD MEYER

WILLIAM WALLACE
1911-12
OIL ON CANVAS
29½ × 24½″
COLLECTION IDAHO STATE HISTORICAL SOCIETY

CALEB LYON
1911-12
OIL ON CANVAS
29½ × 24½″
COLLECTION IDAHO STATE HISTORICAL SOCIETY

FRANK STEUNENBERG
1911-12
OIL ON CANVAS
29½ × 24½″
COLLECTION IDAHO STATE HISTORICAL SOCIETY

JAMES H. HAWLEY
1911-12
OIL ON CANVAS
29¼ × 24½″
COLLECTION IDAHO STATE HISTORICAL SOCIETY

E. CROMBE
NUDE WOMEN
CIRCA 1890
OIL ON CANVAS
25 × 30″
COLLECTION IDAHO STATE HISTORICAL SOCIETY

HENRY L. A. CULMER
SHOSHONE FALLS
CIRCA 1900
OIL ON CANVAS
13 × 26″
COLLECTION MUSEUM OF CHURCH HISTORY AND ART
SALT LAKE CITY

KIRTLAND KELSEY CUTTER
IDAHO STATE BUILDING FOR THE WORLD'S COLUMBIAN EXPOSITION
1892
INK WASH ON PAPER
19¾ × 31¾″
COLLECTION LARRY SCHOONOVER

WILMA DENTON
ROSES
CIRCA 1890
OIL ON CANVAS
16 × 20″
COLLECTION DALE WALDEN

ALF DUNN
WORLD WAR II STUDENT HOUSING
MID 1940s
WATERCOLOR ON PAPER
12½ × 19¼″
COLLECTION LATAH COUNTY HISTORICAL SOCIETY

BRICK PLANT, 8TH STREET, MOSCOW
1943
WATERCOLOR ON PAPER
13⅝ × 19⅛″
COLLECTION LATAH COUNTY HISTORICAL SOCIETY

MOSCOW RAILROAD YARDS
1951
WATERCOLOR ON PAPER
12¾ × 19⅞″
COLLECTION LATAH COUNTY HISTORICAL SOCIETY

W. W. ELLIOTT
HISTORY OF IDAHO TERRITORY
1884
ORIGINAL EDITION OF BOOK
14 × 11 × 1½″
COLLECTION IDAHO STATE HISTORICAL SOCIETY
LIBRARY AND ARCHIVES

LUMBER AND FLOUR MILLS, & MT. IDAHO RANCH
1884
LITHOGRAPH
8⅜ × 11½″
COURTESY CAROLYN STALEY FINE PRINTS
SEATTLE, WASHINGTON

HUGH C. CLAWSON'S RESIDENCE AND TOLL GATE, 7 MILES FROM BOISE CITY, ON IDAHO ROAD
1884
LITHOGRAPH
9 × 12¼″
COURTESY CAROLYN STALEY FINE PRINTS
SEATTLE, WASHINGTON

BIRD'S-EYE VIEW OF GRIME'S CREEK & VICINITY
1884
LITHOGRAPH
8½ × 11⅞″
COURTESY CAROLYN STALEY FINE PRINTS
SEATTLE, WASHINGTON

BIRD'S-EYE VIEW OF KETCHUM
1884
LITHOGRAPH
8¾ × 11½″
COURTESY CAROLYN STALEY FINE PRINTS
SEATTLE, WASHINGTON

THE GUYER HOT SPRINGS.
I. I. LEWIS MANAGER.
2 MILES WEST OF KETCHUM.
ALTURAS CO. IDAHO
1884
LITHOGRAPH
8½ × 11⅜″
COURTESY CAROLYN STALEY FINE PRINTS
SEATTLE, WASHINGTON

REEVES EULER
HEAD OF A WOMAN
1947
SANDSTONE SCULPTURE
21½ × 11 × 8″
COLLECTION BOISE ART MUSEUM

CORNELIA HART FARRER
APPLE ORCHARD
CIRCA 1940
OIL ON BOARD
17 × 18½″
COURTESY OF THE ARTIST

PEACEFUL COVE
CIRCA 1950
OIL ON BOARD
23¾ × 17¾″
COLLECTION IDAHO CITY HISTORICAL FOUNDATION, INC.

JOHN FERY
LAKE PEND OREILLE, IDAHO
1892
OIL ON CANVAS
45 × 80″
COLLECTION BURLINGTON RESOURCES

MINNIE FINNIGAN
HUNTER AND DOGS
CIRCA 1910
PENCIL ON PAPER
16½ × 25″
COLLECTION IDAHO STATE HISTORICAL SOCIETY

PATRICK FLAMMIA
LOG JAMMER
1950
OIL ON CANVAS BOARD
11⅝ × 15½″
COLLECTION CHENEY COWLES MUSEUM

MARY HALLOCK FOOTE
A PRETTY GIRL IN THE WEST
CENTURY MAGAZINE
OCTOBER, 1889
PENCIL AND WASH ON PAPER
5½ × 7⅞″
COLLECTION LIBRARY OF CONGRESS
WASHINGTON, D.C.

BETWEEN THE DESERT AND THE SOWN
CENTURY MAGAZINE
MAY, 1895
PENCIL AND WASH ON PAPER
6⅞ × 10″
COLLECTION LIBRARY OF CONGRESS
WASHINGTON, D.C.

ETHEL FOWLER
PORTRAIT
CIRCA 1930
WATERCOLOR ON PAPER
16 × 13″
COLLECTION BOISE ART MUSEUM

FATHER
1933
WATERCOLOR ON PAPER
10 × 8″
COLLECTION BOISE ART MUSEUM

ONIONS
1937
WATERCOLOR ON PAPER
9¾ × 15″
COLLECTION BOISE ART MUSEUM

FRANK LESLIE'S ILLUSTRATED NEWSPAPER
OUR ARTIST'S WANDERINGS IN THE FAR WEST—THE FIRST WOMAN IN CAMP IN THE COEUR D'ALENE MINING DISTRICT, IDAHO
VOL. 57, NO. 1491.
WEEK ENDING APRIL 19, 1884. COVER PAGE.
LITHOGRAPH
15½ × 10⅞″
COLLECTION IDAHO STATE HISTORICAL SOCIETY
LIBRARY AND ARCHIVES

GEORGE GIBBS
SHOSHONE FALLS OF SNAKE RIVER
AUG. 15, 1849, FROM BELOW
PENCIL ON PAPER
5⅜ × 8⅜″
COLLECTION PEABODY MUSEUM OF ARCHAEOLOGY AND ETHNOLOGY, HARVARD UNIVERSITY

GILBERT
BOISE-ROCHESTER MILL, ATLANTA
1916-17
OIL ON CANVAS
24½ × 29¼″
COLLECTION IDAHO STATE HISTORICAL SOCIETY

U. L. GRAY
PACKER JOHN'S CABIN
CIRCA 1910
OIL ON CANVAS
19⅝ × 27½″
COLLECTION IDAHO STATE HISTORICAL SOCIETY

IDAHO PEARS
1910
OIL ON CANVAS
14¼ × 30¾″
COLLECTION BETTY PENSON-WARD

IDAHO'S BOUNTY
1910
OIL ON CANVAS
19¼ × 35½″
COLLECTION BETTY PENSON-WARD

EMMA EDWARDS GREEN
THE ROAD TO ROCKY BAR
CIRCA 1890
OIL ON CANVAS
12½ × 16½″
COLLECTION IDAHO STATE HISTORICAL SOCIETY

ROSES
1890
OIL ON CANVAS
26¼ × 16⅜″
COLLECTION IDAHO STATE HISTORICAL SOCIETY

WHEN EVENING SHADOWS FALL ON THE LOON CREEK TRAIL
CIRCA 1890
WATERCOLOR ON PAPER
9[illegible] × 11[illegible]″
COLLECTION IDAHO STATE HISTORICAL SOCIETY

STATE SEAL OF IDAHO
1892
OIL ON CANVAS
30 × 30″
COLLECTION IDAHO STATE HISTORICAL SOCIETY

MT. CUDDY ON WEISER RIVER
1892-93
OIL ON CANVAS
15 1/2 × 19 3/8″
COLLECTION IDAHO STATE HISTORICAL SOCIETY

OLD MILL AT HEATH MINING DISTRICT
1893
OIL ON CANVAS
19 3/8 × 23 3/8″
COLLECTION IDAHO STATE HISTORICAL SOCIETY

EDMOND GREENE
ATLANTA, ALTURAS COUNTRY, IDAHO
CIRCA 1880
LITHOGRAPH BY HENRY STEINEGGER
15 7/16 × 20 1/2″
COLLECTION AMON CARTER MUSEUM, FORT WORTH

ATLANTA MINE, ATLANTA, IDAHO
CIRCA 1880
LITHOGRAPH BY HENRY STEINEGGER
14 × 20 3/16″
COLLECTION AMON CARTER MUSEUM, FORT WORTH

GOLD HILL MINE & WORKS, QUARTZBURG, BOISE CO., IDAHO
CIRCA 1880
LITHOGRAPH BY HENRY STEINEGGER
11 3/4 × 31 5/8″
COLLECTION AMON CARTER MUSEUM, FORT WORTH

SHOSHONE TWIN FALLS OF SNAKE RIVER 190 FEET HIGH, CASSIA COUNTY, IDAHO
CIRCA 1880
LITHOGRAPH BY HENRY STEINEGGER
14 1/4 × 20″
COLLECTION IDAHO STATE HISTORICAL SOCIETY

HARPER'S WEEKLY
NEZ PERCE CAMPAIGNS, FROM SKETCHES BY VINCENT COLYER
AUGUST 18, 1877, P. 641
LITHOGRAPH
15 1/2 × 10 3/4″
COLLECTION IDAHO STATE HISTORICAL SOCIETY
LIBRARY AND ARCHIVES

DEAD MULE TRAIL, FROM A SKETCH BY AN ARMY OFFICER
SEPTEMBER 29, 1877, COVER PAGE
LITHOGRAPH
15 3/8 × 10 7/8″
COLLECTION IDAHO STATE HISTORICAL SOCIETY
LIBRARY AND ARCHIVES

NEZ PERCES WAR, FROM SKETCHES BY AN ARMY OFFICER
OCTOBER 27, 1877, P. 840
LITHOGRAPH
15 1/2 × 10 3/4″
COLLECTION IDAHO STATE HISTORICAL SOCIETY
LIBRARY AND ARCHIVES

END OF THE NEZ PERCE WAR, SURRENDER OF CHIEF JOSEPH, FROM SKETCHES IN THE FIELD
NOVEMBER 17, 1877, P. 905
LITHOGRAPH
15 1/2 × 10 3/4″
COLLECTION IDAHO STATE HISTORICAL SOCIETY
LIBRARY AND ARCHIVES

FRANK JAY HAYNES
UP MAIN STREET, BURKE, IDAHO
1893
CONTACT PRINT FROM ORIGINAL GLASS NEGATIVE
11 × 14″
COURTESY MONTANA HISTORICAL SOCIETY

W. J. PILLING GROUP (ALL R.R. BOYS), HOPE, IDAHO
1890
CONTACT PRINT FROM ORIGINAL GLASS NEGATIVE
11 × 14″
COURTESY MONTANA HISTORICAL SOCIETY

ABBY WILLIAMS HILL
CABINET GORGE, IDAHO
1904
OIL ON CANVAS
38 × 28″
COLLECTION UNIVERSITY OF PUGET SOUND

VERMILLION CLIFFS, HELL GATE CANYON
1906
OIL ON CANVAS
38 × 28″
COLLECTION UNIVERSITY OF PUGET SOUND

ARM HINCELIN
MAIN STREET, BOISE
1864
OIL ON CANVAS
12 × 20″
COLLECTION IDAHO STATE HISTORICAL SOCIETY

MERRITT DANA HOUGHTON
MULLAN, IDAHO
1907
PEN AND INK ON PAPER
17 × 26 1/4″
COLLECTION CHENEY COWLES MUSEUM

MARIE ISABELLA DUFFIELD IRVIN
STILL LIFE WITH AMERICAN ART POTTERY
1892
OIL ON CANVAS
20 × 24″
COLLECTION DALE WALDEN

IDAHO LANDSCAPE
CIRCA 1910
OIL ON CANVAS
16 × 24″
COLLECTION DALE WALDEN

MRS. HART'S BACK YARD
CIRCA 1910
OIL ON PANEL
13 3/4 × 9 3/4″
COLLECTION DALE WALDEN

DESIGN FOR A RUG
CIRCA 1920s
WATERCOLOR ON PAPER
12 × 18″
COLLECTION COLLEGE OF IDAHO
ROSENTHAL GALLERY OF ART

OAK LEAVES
CIRCA 1920s
PENCIL & WATERCOLOR ON PAPER
19¾ × 14″
COLLECTION COLLEGE OF IDAHO
ROSENTHAL GALLERY OF ART

SILK PATTERN FLORAL DESIGN
CIRCA 1920s
WATERCOLOR ON PAPER
12 × 12″
COLLECTION COLLEGE OF IDAHO
ROSENTHAL GALLERY OF ART

JULIAN E. ITTER
MINERS AND CABIN
CIRCA 1900
OIL ON CANVAS
11½ × 16¼″
COLLECTION CHENEY COWLES MUSEUM

WILLIAM HENRY JACKSON
FORT HALL, IDAHO
CIRCA 1930
WATERCOLOR ON PAPER
9½ × 14¼″
COLLECTION BUFFALO BILL HISTORICAL CENTER
CODY, WYOMING

FRANK TENNEY JOHNSON
COWBOY, POCATELLO, IDAHO
1909
WATERCOLOR ON PAPER
7 × 5″
COLLECTION JOHN C. HOOVER

MARY KIRKWOOD
KATHRYN KENNARD VAUGHT
1948
OIL ON CANVAS
48 × 38″
COLLECTION UNIVERSITY OF IDAHO
LIONEL HAMPTON SCHOOL OF MUSIC

WHEAT STUBBLE
1948
OIL ON CANVAS
23¾ × 33″
COLLECTION UNIVERSITY OF IDAHO
LIONEL HAMPTON SCHOOL OF MUSIC

NELLIE KILGORE KLINGE
ZINNIAS
1937
OIL ON PANEL
28 × 21″
COLLECTION BOISE ART MUSEUM

AUGUSTUS KOCH
BIRD'S EYE VIEW OF BOISE CITY, ADA COUNTY, THE CAPITAL OF IDAHO
ATTRIBUTED TO AUGUSTUS KOCH
CIRCA 1890
LITHOGRAPH
24½ × 32″
COLLECTION BOISE PUBLIC LIBRARY

BIRD'S EYE VIEW OF THE CITY OF MOSCOW, LATAH COUNTY, IDAHO
1897
LITHOGRAPH
24 × 32″
COLLECTION UNIVERSITY OF IDAHO LIBRARY

MINNIE TAYLOR LAUDER
COWS BY A POND
1888
OIL ON CANVAS
24 × 33⅝″
COLLECTION LATAH COUNTY HISTORICAL SOCIETY

ROBERT W. LIMBERT
ELK
CIRCA 1915
OIL ON CANVAS
32 × 40″
COLLECTION IDAHO STATE HISTORICAL SOCIETY

CALEB LYON
SEAL OF IDAHO COAT OF ARMS [TERRITORIAL SEAL]
1866
PENCIL ON PAPER
4½ × 3¼″
COLLECTION UNIVERSITY OF IDAHO LIBRARY

MR. AND MRS. WALTER H. MCINTOSH
SOLIDER CANYON NEAR FORT LAPWAI
1886
OIL ON CANVAS
27¾ × 23¾″
COLLECTION UNIVERSITY OF IDAHO LIBRARY

JOSEPH P. MCMEEKIN
PIONEER WOMAN WITH BRASS BUCKETS
1901
OIL ON CANVAS
18⅛ × 12¼″
COLLECTION IDAHO STATE HISTORICAL SOCIETY

HAGERMAN VIA BLISS, IDAHO
1903
OIL ON CANVAS
19½ × 30¼″
COLLECTION IDAHO STATE HISTORICAL SOCIETY

WOOD GATHERING (MILLET ISLAND, IDAHO)
1907
OIL ON CANVAS
24 × 16″
COLLECTION MR. AND MRS. PHILIP FAST

GEMS OF THE DESERT
1909
OIL ON CANVAS
24 × 36″
COLLECTION IDAHO STATE HISTORICAL SOCIETY

BRUSH GATHERERS ON MILLET ISLAND
1910
OIL ON CANVAS
13¾ × 23¾″
COLLECTION IDAHO STATE HISTORICAL SOCIETY

PATCHWORK QUILT
1910
OIL ON CANVAS
18 × 11¾″
COLLECTION IDAHO STATE HISTORICAL SOCIETY

REGAL SHOSHONE
1910
OIL ON CANVAS
24 × 36″
COLLECTION IDAHO STATE HISTORICAL SOCIETY

FLETCHER MARTIN
MINE RESCUE
STUDY FOR MURAL FOR KELLOGG, IDAHO
1939
TEMPERA ON PANEL
15 × 36″
NATIONAL MUSEUM OF AMERICAN ART,
SMITHSONIAN INSTITUTION,
TRANSFER FROM GENERAL SERVICES ADMINISTRATION
COURTESY UNIVERSITY OF MARYLAND COLLEGE PARK

CONAN MATHEWS
LANDSCAPE
1948
OIL ON MASONITE
27¼ × 23½″
COLLECTION CHENEY COWLES MUSEUM

ALFRED JACOB MILLER
PIERRE—A ROCKY MOUNTAIN TRAPPER
CIRCA 1837
PENCIL, PEN, INK, WASH & GOUACHE ON PAPER
6¾ × 9¾″
COLLECTION THE THOMAS GILCREASE INSTITUTE
OF AMERICAN HISTORY AND ART, TULSA, OKLAHOMA

SNAKE INDIAN
CIRCA 1837
PENCIL AND WATERCOLOR ON PAPER
5½ × 4½″
COLLECTION BUFFALO BILL HISTORICAL CENTER
CODY, WYOMING
BEQUEST OF JOSEPH M. ROEBLING

OLAF MOLLER
STREET SCENE, ALBION
1934
OIL ON CANVAS
20 × 24″
COLLECTION BOISE ART MUSEUM

UNION PACIFIC DEPOT
1934
OIL ON CANVAS
20 × 24″
COLLECTION BOISE ART MUSEUM

BLUE VASE
CIRCA 1935
OIL ON CANVAS
24 × 24″
COLLECTION DALE WALDEN

AGNES RANDALL MOORE
HEAD OF A WOMAN
CIRCA 1930
INK ON MATBOARD
10½ × 8″
COLLECTION LATAH COUNTY HISTORICAL SOCIETY

FLORAL MOTIF
CIRCA 1930
INK ON MATBOARD
10½ × 8″
COLLECTION LATAH COUNTY HISTORICAL SOCIETY

TWO WOMEN IN SUITS
CIRCA 1930
INK ON MATBOARD
10½ × 8″
COLLECTION LATAH COUNTY HISTORICAL SOCIETY

PETER MORAN
THE TETONS
1879
WATERCOLOR ON PAPER
12 × 18″
COLLECTION ROSWELL MUSEUM & ART CENTER
GIFT OF SENATOR CLINTON P. ANDERSON

THOMAS MORAN
PORT NEUF CANYON, IDAHO
1873
WATERCOLOR OVER GRAPHITE ON PAPER
3 × 5½″
COOPER-HEWITT MUSEUM, THE SMITHSONIAN INSTITUTION'S
NATIONAL MUSEUM OF DESIGN

FORT HALL, IDAHO
1879
WATERCOLOR AND PENCIL ON PAPER
7 × 10½″
COLLECTION NATIONAL PARK SERVICE
GRAND TETON NATIONAL PARK

PORT NEUF CANYON, IDAHO
1879
PENCIL & WATERCOLOR ON PAPER
12 × 20″
COLLECTION THE THOMAS GILCREASE INSTITUTE
OF AMERICAN HISTORY AND ART, TULSA, OKLAHOMA

SHOSHONE FALLS, IDAHO
1879
GRAPHITE ON BLUE-GREY WOVE PAPER
10½ × 14½″
COOPER-HEWITT MUSEUM, THE SMITHSONIAN INSTITUTION'S
NATIONAL MUSEUM OF DESIGN

THE TETONS, IDAHO
1879
GRAPHITE AND WATERCOLOR ON GREY LAID PAPER
8¼ × 14⅜″
COOPER-HEWITT MUSEUM, THE SMITHSONIAN INSTITUTION'S
NATIONAL MUSEUM OF DESIGN

THE TETONS, IDAHO
1879
INK WASH ON PAPER
14 × 10″
COLLECTION NATIONAL PARK SERVICE
GRAND TETON NATIONAL PARK

SHOSHONE TEPEE
1892
GRAPHITE AND WASH ON PAPER
5⅜ × 7½″
COLLECTION PEABODY MUSEUM OF ARCHAEOLOGY AND
ETHNOLOGY, HARVARD UNIVERSITY

BLUE LAKES, IDAHO
1900
PENCIL & WATERCOLOR ON PAPER
10¾ × 15″
COLLECTION THE THOMAS GILCREASE INSTITUTE
OF AMERICAN HISTORY AND ART, TULSA, OKLAHOMA

THOMAS RAYMOND NEILSON
WINTER ON PORTNEUF
CIRCA 1940
OIL ON CANVAS
15 × 20″
IDAHO STATE UNIVERSITY
STUDENT UNION PERMANENT ART COLLECTION

THE COTTONWOOD
CIRCA 1940
OIL ON CANVAS
24½ × 29″
PRIVATE COLLECTION

CHARLES OSTNER
BOISE CITY
1903
MIXED MEDIA ON PAPER
16 × 20″
COLLECTION IDAHO STATE HISTORICAL SOCIETY

BOISE CITY, PRINCIPAL BUSINESS HOUSES AND PRIVATE RESIDENCES
CIRCA 1879
LITHOGRAPH
20 × 26″
COLLECTION BOISE PUBLIC LIBRARY

THE SCOUT (PORTRAIT OF LAWMAN RUBE ROBBINS)
N.D.
OIL ON CANVAS
25½ × 23⅜″
COLLECTION IDAHO STATE HISTORICAL SOCIETY

HERD OF WILD HORSES
1903
WATERCOLOR ON PAPER
19 × 24″
COLLECTION IDAHO STATE HISTORICAL SOCIETY

LEAVING FOR DEADWOOD
CIRCA 1865
OIL ON CANVAS
26⅝ × 33⅜″
COLLECTION IDAHO STATE HISTORICAL SOCIETY

EX-GOVERNOR FRANK STEUNENBERG
CIRCA 1900-1910
OIL ON CANVAS
38¼ × 24¼″
COLLECTION IDAHO STATE HISTORICAL SOCIETY

BEAR'S ATTACK
CIRCA 1865
OIL ON CANVAS
26⅛ × 33⅜″
COLLECTION IDAHO STATE HISTORICAL SOCIETY

FRANK PALMER
THE NARROWS AT TWIN LAKES, IDAHO
CIRCA 1912
SEPIA TONED PRINT
10½ × 13½″
COURTESY EASTERN WASHINGTON STATE HISTORICAL SOCIETY

ST. MARIES
CIRCA 1910
SEPIA TONED PRINT
10½ × 13½″
COURTESY EASTERN WASHINGTON STATE HISTORICAL SOCIETY

DEPOT AT TWIN LAKES
CIRCA 1910
SEPIA TONED PRINT
10½ × 13½″
COURTESY EASTERN WASHINGTON STATE HISTORICAL SOCIETY

HARRY PARNELL
JAMES HOGAN
1948
OIL ON BOARD
11¼ × 9″
COLLECTION IDAHO STATE HISTORICAL SOCIETY

ELLA PARRISH
PIONEER HOME OF DOUGLAS KNOX AND FAMILY, 1872
1883
OIL ON CANVAS
24 × 36″
COLLECTION IDAHO STATE HISTORICAL SOCIETY

WILLIAM SAMUEL PARROTT
SHOSHONE FALLS
1885
OIL ON CANVAS
19¾ × 29⅝″
COLLECTION MR. AND MRS. JOHN KIRBY

OLIVER PARSON
OLD MERRIT RANCH
1958
OIL ON MASONITE
23½ × 35½″
COLLECTION BOISE ART MUSEUM

NICOLAS POINT
DESCENTE DIFFICILE
1841
GRAPHITE ON PAPER
3½ × 6″
PIERRE JEAN DE SMET PAPERS
COLLECTION WASHINGTON STATE UNIVERSITY LIBRARIES

DESERTE ARIDE
1841
GRAPHITE ON PAPER
3 × 6″
PIERRE JEAN DE SMET PAPERS
COLLECTION WASHINGTON STATE UNIVERSITY LIBRARIES

FAMILLE SERPENTE EN VOYAGE
1841
GRAPHITE ON PAPER
3 × 5½″
PIERRE JEAN DE SMET PAPERS
COLLECTION WASHINGTON STATE UNIVERSITY LIBRARIES

INTERIEUR DE L'EGLISE DU SACRE COEUR CHEZ LES COEUR D'ALENES
1842
WATERCOLOR, PENCIL AND INK ON PAPER
4½ × 6½″
PIERRE JEAN DE SMET PAPERS
COLLECTION WASHINGTON STATE UNIVERSITY LIBRARIES

VIGILANCE - COURAGE - NAIVETE
CIRCA 1841-44
GRAPHITE ON PAPER
4⅞ × 5½″
PIERRE JEAN DE SMET PAPERS
COLLECTION WASHINGTON STATE UNIVERSITY LIBRARIES

VIEW OF THE NEW MISSION ESTABLISHMENT IN 1846 AMONG THE POINTED-HEARTS
1846
GRAPHITE ON PAPER
5 × 7½″
PIERRE JEAN DE SMET PAPERS
COLLECTION WASHINGTON STATE UNIVERSITY LIBRARIES

INDIAN MODE OF TRAVELLING
CIRCA 1846
ENGRAVING
3½ × 6″
PIERRE JEAN DE SMET PAPERS
COLLECTION WASHINGTON STATE UNIVERSITY LIBRARIES

VIEW OF THE MISSION ESTABLISHMENT IN 1846 AMONG THE POINTED-HEARTS
1846
ENGRAVING
4½ × 7½″
PIERRE JEAN DE SMET PAPERS
COLLECTION WASHINGTON STATE UNIVERSITY LIBRARIES

KATHERINE POSTLE
THE MALAD CANYON
CIRCA 1925
OIL ON PANEL
25¼ × 35¼″
COLLECTION BOISE ART MUSEUM

CHARLES PREUSS
AMERICAN FALLS OF LEWIS FORK
1845
LITHOGRAPH
5 × 7½″
COLLECTION IDAHO STATE HISTORICAL SOCIETY
LIBRARY AND ARCHIVES

H. S. RAYBURN
DESERT STAGE STATION ON OLD OREGON TRAIL AT ROCK CREEK CANYON NEAR TWIN FALLS, IDAHO
N.D.
PEN AND INK ON PAPER
16 × 27″
COLLECTION IDAHO STATE HISTORICAL SOCIETY

FREDERIC REMINGTON
REGISTER ROCK, IDAHO
ATTRIBUTED TO FREDERIC REMINGTON
1891
OIL ON CANVAS
17⅛ × 27¾″
COLLECTION AMON CARTER MUSEUM, FORT WORTH

AGNES BOWEN RICHTER
WALTER'S FERRY ON SNAKE RIVER
1890
OIL ON CANVAS
10¼ × 18″
COLLECTION IDAHO STATE HISTORICAL SOCIETY

GEORGE ROBERTS
DOGS OF WAR
CIRCA 1950
WELDED IRON
21 × 10 × 33″
COLLECTION WILLIAM AND GENEVRA SLOAN

GEORGE SCHROEDER
MORNING BLUSH IN THE SAWTOOTHS
CIRCA 1920
OIL ON CANVAS
13½ × 35″
COLLECTION JOHN P. BLANCHARD

MISTY MORNING ON THE RIVER, HEYBURN, IDAHO
CIRCA 1920
OIL ON CANVAS
10 × 12″
COLLECTION MR. AND MRS. FRANK BLANCHARD

WOOD RIVER
CIRCA 1920s
OIL ON CANVAS
10 × 15½″
COLLECTION MR. AND MRS. FRANK BLANCHARD

BAKER CREEK, HIDDEN VALLEY
CIRCA 1920s
OIL ON CANVAS
9½ × 13″
COLLECTION MR. AND MRS. FRANK BLANCHARD

OCTOBER SUNNY LANE, HAGERMAN
1913
OIL ON CANVAS
9⅝ × 6½″
COLLECTION MR. AND MRS. FRANK BLANCHARD

GEORGE E. SHIPLEY
SENATOR BORAH
CIRCA 1930s
PENCIL ON PAPER
12 × 8″
COLLECTION IDAHO STATE HISTORICAL SOCIETY

SENATOR BORAH
CIRCA 1930s
PENCIL ON PAPER
12 × 8″
COLLECTION IDAHO STATE HISTORICAL SOCIETY

NELL SHIPMAN
TRAIL OF THE NORTH WIND
1923
16MM BLACK & WHITE SILENT FILM
RUNNING TIME 20 MINUTES
IDAHO FILM COLLECTION
HEMINGWAY WESTERN STUDIES CENTER
BOISE STATE UNIVERSITY

THE LIGHT ON LOOKOUT
1923
16MM BLACK & WHITE SILENT FILM
RUNNING TIME 18 MINUTES
IDAHO FILM COLLECTION
HEMINGWAY WESTERN STUDIES CENTER
BOISE STATE UNIVERSITY

T. SLIGHT
GROVE STREET IN BOISE
1897
OIL ON CANVAS
29¼ × 44½″
COLLECTION IDAHO STATE HISTORICAL SOCIETY

CECIL SMITH
TWENTY MULE TEAM
1934
OIL ON CANVAS
25 × 48″
COLLECTION IDAHO STATE HISTORICAL SOCIETY

A LITTLE MIXUP
1939
DRY BRUSH ON PAPER
10¾ × 20″
COLLECTION BOISE ART MUSEUM

EDWARD SMITH
SEVEN DEVILS MOUNTAINS
1893
OIL ON CANVAS
41¼ × 53¼″
COLLECTION IDAHO STATE HISTORICAL SOCIETY

W. THOMAS SMITH
MRS. CHARLOTTE FINCH, HAYDEN LAKE
1906
OIL ON CANVAS
38 × 27½″
COLLECTION CHENEY COWLES MUSEUM

GUSTAVUS SOHON
NEZ PERCE ARRIVING AT WALLA WALLA COUNCIL
1855
PENCIL ON PAPER
8 × 12″
COLLECTION NATIONAL ANTHROPOLOGICAL ARCHIVES
SMITHSONIAN INSTITUTION

NEZ PERCE MAKING RECORD OF COUNCIL
1855
PENCIL ON PAPER
8 × 12″
COLLECTION NATIONAL ANTHROPOLOGICAL ARCHIVES
SMITHSONIAN INSTITUTION

KAMAS PRAIRIE OF THE PEND D'OREILLES INDIANS
1858
COLOR LITHOGRAPH
6 × 9¼″
COLLECTION IDAHO STATE HISTORICAL SOCIETY
LIBRARY AND ARCHIVES

COEUR D'ALENE MISSION IN THE ROCKY MOUNTAINS
1863
LITHOGRAPH
5 × 8½″
COLLECTION IDAHO STATE HISTORICAL SOCIETY
LIBRARY AND ARCHIVES

ELIZA SPALDING
ARRIVAL OF THE WHITMAN-SPALDING PARTY AT THE SUMMIT OF THE ROCKIES
COPY BY UNKNOWN ARTIST
N.D.
OIL ON CANVAS
9½ × 13½″
HENRY AND ELIZA SPALDING PAPERS
COLLECTION WASHINGTON STATE UNIVERSITY LIBRARIES

SAMUEL SPIELMAN
STILL LIFE
1935
OIL ON CANVAS
37¾ × 31¾″
COLLECTION BOISE ART MUSEUM

JOHN MIX STANLEY
ON THE SNAKE RIVER
CIRCA 1850
OIL ON CANVAS
36 × 54″
COURTESY KENNEDY GALLERIES, INC., NEW YORK

COEUR D'ALENE MISSION, ST. IGNATIUS RIVER [SIC]
1855
COLOR LITHOGRAPH
6¼ × 9¼″
COLLECTION IDAHO STATE HISTORICAL SOCIETY
LIBRARY AND ARCHIVES

NEZ PERCES
1855
COLOR LITHOGRAPH
6¼ × 9¼″
COLLECTION JUDGE ALFRED C. HAGAN

HERBERT MORTON STOOPS
CONFRONTATION
CIRCA 1920s
OIL ON CANVAS
32 × 36″
COURTESY SIDESTREET GALLERY
SANDPOINT, IDAHO

GRANVILLE STUART
FORT HALL
1857
PENCIL ON NOTE PAPER
10 × 9″
COLLECTION MUSEUM OF NATIVE
AMERICAN CULTURES, SPOKANE

JAMES EVERETT STUART
LOOKING OVER THE TOP OF SHOSHONE FALLS, IDAHO
JUNE 1885
OIL ON CANVAS
18 × 30″
COURTESY SIDESTREET GALLERY
SANDPOINT, IDAHO

WILLIAM TAPPAN
OUTSIDE VIEW OF FORT BOISE
1850
LITHOGRAPH
6⅜ × 8⅞″
COLLECTION IDAHO STATE HISTORICAL SOCIETY
LIBRARY AND ARCHIVES

INSIDE VIEW OF FORT BOISE ON SNAKE RIVER
1850
LITHOGRAPH
5 × 8″
COLLECTION IDAHO STATE HISTORICAL SOCIETY
LIBRARY AND ARCHIVES

OUTSIDE VIEW OF FORT HALL
1850
LITHOGRAPH
5¼ × 8¾″
COLLECTION IDAHO STATE HISTORICAL SOCIETY
LIBRARY AND ARCHIVES

INSIDE VIEW OF FORT HALL
1850
LITHOGRAPH
5 × 8″
COLLECTION IDAHO STATE HISTORICAL SOCIETY
LIBRARY AND ARCHIVES

ARCHIE BOYD TEATER
PINK LILY POND
CIRCA 1950s
OIL ON CANVAS
30 × 50″
COLLECTION LARRY MEIEROTTO AND MARY ABERCROMBIE
COURTESY YATES-FRITCHMAN GALLERIES

TEATER STUDIO GARDEN
CIRCA 1950s
OIL ON CANVAS
26 × 40″
COLLECTION LARRY MEIEROTTO AND MARY ABERCROMBIE
COURTESY YATES-FRITCHMAN GALLERIES

MINERVA TEICHERT
OX DRAWN WAGON FORDING CREEK
CIRCA 1940
OIL ON CANVAS
18½ × 48″
IDAHO STATE UNIVERSITY
STUDENT UNION PERMANENT ART COLLECTION

TOURTELLOTTE AND HUMMEL, ARCHITECTS
UNIVERSITY OF IDAHO ADMINISTRATION BUILDING
TOURTELLOTTE AND COMPANY, ARCHITECTS
PRESENTATION DRAWING BY M. HALLOWELL
1908
INK ON PAPER
22 × 30″
COURTESY HUMMEL, LAMARCHE & HUNSUCKER, ARCHITECTS, P.A.

IDAHO STATE CAPITOL
TOURTELLOTTE AND COMPANY, ARCHITECTS
PRESENTATION DRAWING
1909
GRAPHITE, INK AND WATERCOLOR ON BOARD
51½ × 38¾″
COURTESY HUMMEL, LAMARCHE & HUNSUCKER, ARCHITECTS, P.A.

HOTEL BOISE
TOURTELLOTTE AND HUMMEL, ARCHITECTS
1929-30
CHARCOAL WASH ON CARDBOARD
17 × 11½″
COURTESY HUMMEL, LAMARCHE & HUNSUCKER, ARCHITECTS, P.A.

EGYPTIAN THEATRE
TOURTELLOTTE AND HUMMEL, ARCHITECTS
PRESENTATION DRAWING BY FRANK K. HUMMEL
1926
GRAPHITE AND WATERCOLOR ON PAPER
19½ × 29″
COURTESY HUMMEL, LAMARCHE & HUNSUCKER, ARCHITECTS, P.A.

EGYPTIAN THEATRE
TOURTELLOTTE AND HUMMEL, ARCHITECTS
HUGO CLAUSEN & CO., DECORATOR
RENDERING OF INTERIOR
1926
WATERCOLOR AND TEMPERA ON ILLUSTRATION BOARD
31½ × 24¾″
COURTESY HUMMEL, LAMARCHE & HUNSUCKER, ARCHITECTS, P.A.

NICK VILLENEUVE
WILLIAM BYRON HOME, 12TH AND MAIN, BOISE
CIRCA 1920s
PEN AND INK
14 × 21½″
COLLECTION IDAHO STATE HISTORICAL SOCIETY

IDAHO'S GRAND OLD MAN
1923
WATERCOLOR AND INK ON PAPER
27½ × 19½″
COLLECTION IDAHO STATE HISTORICAL SOCIETY

FEODOR VON LUERZER
CABIN POINT
1910
OIL ON BURLAP
28 × 60″
COLLECTION JACK SPURGEON

FOREST FIRE IN NORTH IDAHO WOODS
1910
OIL ON BURLAP
28 × 41″
COLLECTION JACK SPURGEON

ST. JOE RIVER
1910
OIL ON BURLAP
28 × 64″
COLLECTION JACK SPURGEON

ARNOLD WESTERLUND
CARAVELLE — SHIPS IN THE NIGHT
CIRCA 1950s
ETCHING WITH FOUND FORMS
13½ × 12½″
COLLECTION MARCIA ANDERSON
COURTESY OF THE ARTIST

WEST SHORE MAGAZINE
SHOSHONE FALLS, IDAHO
CIRCA 1875-1890s
LITHOGRAPH
[illegible]
COURTESY CAROLYN STALEY FINE PRINTS
SEATTLE, WASHINGTON

IDAHO — FERRYING ACROSS THE SNAKE RIVER
CIRCA 1870-1890s
LITHOGRAPH
7 13/16 × 10¼″
COURTESY CAROLYN STALEY FINE PRINTS
SEATTLE, WASHINGTON

JAMES F. WILKINS
DESCENT OF BEAR RIVER MOUNTAINS AUGUST 1
1849
MONOCHROME WASH DRAWING ON PAPER
8½ × 10″
ICONOGRAPHIC COLLECTIONS
STATE HISTORICAL SOCIETY OF WISCONSIN

BEAR RIVER AUGUST 1
1849
MONOCHROME WASH DRAWING ON PAPER
8½ × 10⅛″
ICONOGRAPHIC COLLECTIONS
STATE HISTORICAL SOCIETY OF WISCONSIN

BEAR MOUNTAINS SUN RISE AUGUST 2
1849
MONOCHROME WASH DRAWING ON PAPER
8½ × 10⅛″
ICONOGRAPHIC COLLECTIONS
STATE HISTORICAL SOCIETY OF WISCONSIN

BEER [SODA] SPRINGS AUGUST 3
1849
MONOCHROME WASH DRAWING ON PAPER
8½ × 20⅛″
ICONOGRAPHIC COLLECTIONS
STATE HISTORICAL SOCIETY OF WISCONSIN

STEAM BOAT SPRINGS AUGUST 4
1849
MONOCHROME WASH DRAWING ON PAPER
8⅜ × 10 3/16″
ICONOGRAPHIC COLLECTIONS
STATE HISTORICAL SOCIETY OF WISCONSIN

SELECTED BIBLIOGRAPHY

BOOKS

Ainsworth, Ed. *The Cowboy in Art*. New York: World Publishing Company, 1968.

American Frontier Life: Early Western Painting and Prints. Issued in conjunction with the exhibition...organized by the Amon Carter Museum and the Buffalo Bill Historical Center. New York: Abbeville Press, 1987.

Appleton, Marion Brymner. *Who's Who in Northwest Art*. Seattle: Frank McCaffrey, 1941.

An Art Perspective of the Historical Pacific Northwest; from the Collection of Dr. and Mrs. Franz R. Stenzel, Portland, Oregon. Helena: Montana Historical Society, 1963.

Brown, Robert L. *Saloons of the American West*. Silverton, Colorado: Sundance Books, 1978.

Burns, Robert Ignatius. *The Jesuits and the Indian Wars of the Northwest*. New Haven: Yale University Press, 1966.

Catlin, George. *Episodes from* Life Among the Indians *and* Last Rambles. Ed. by Marvin C. Ross. Norman: University of Oklahoma Press, 1959.

Clark, Carol. *Thomas Moran; Watercolors of the American West*. Published for the Amon Carter Museum of Western Art. Austin: University of Texas Press, 1980.

Collins, Alfred and Ethel. *Herbert A. Collins: From Artist to Farmer*. Unpublished essay, 1979. Manuscript collection, Idaho State Historical Society Publications Office, Boise.

Conley, Cort. *Idaho For The Curious; A Guide*. Cambridge, Idaho: Backeddy Books, 1982.

Cross, Osborne. *The March of the Mounted Riflemen...As Recorded in the Journals of Major Osborne Cross and George Gibbs, and the Official Report of Colonel Loring*. Ed. by Raymond W. Settle. Northwest Historical Series, no. 3. Glendale, California: Arthur H. Clark Company, 1940.

Curry, Larry. *The American West; Painters from Catlin to Russell*. New York: Viking, 1972.

Dawdy, Doris Ostrander. *Artists of the American West; A Biographical Dictionary*. 3 volumes. Chicago: Sage Books, 1974-1985.

Erdoes, Richard. *Saloons of the Old West*. New York: Knopf, 1979.

Fields, Ronald M. *Abby Williams Hill and the Lure of the West*. Tacoma: Washington State Historical Society, 1988.

Glanz, Dawn. *How the West Was Drawn: American Art and the Settling of the Frontier*. Madison, Wisconsin: UMI Research Press, 1982.

Goetzmann, William H., and William N. Goetzmann. *Looking at the Land of Promise; Pioneer Images of the Pacific Northwest*. Pullman: Washington State University Press, 1988.

Goetzmann, William H., and Joseph C. Porter. *The West as Romantic Horizon*. Omaha, Nebraska: Center for Western Studies, Joslyn Art Museum / InterNorth Art Foundation, 1981.

Goetzmann, William H., and William N. Goetzmann. *The West of the Imagination*. New York: Norton, 1986.

Haines, Aubrey L. *Historic Sites Along the Oregon Trail*. Gerald, Missouri: Patrice Press, 1981.

Hales, Peter P. *William Henry Jackson and the Transformation of the American Landscape*. Philadelphia: Temple University Press, 1988.

Harrell, Ida Purdy. *Sketch on Merritt D. Houghton and Fannie Houghton*. Unpublished essay, Wyoming State Historical Research and Publications Division, Cheyenne.

Hart, Patricia, and Ivar Nelson. *Mining Town: The Photographic Record of T. N. Barnard and Nellie Stockbridge from the Coeur d'Alenes*. Seattle: University of Washington Press / Boise: Idaho State Historical Society, 1984.

Harthorn, Sandy. *A Voice of Silence; A Restrospective of Works by James Castle*. Boise: Boise Gallery of Art, 1982.

Haseltine, James L. *One Hundred Years of Utah Painting; Selected Works from the 1840s to the 1940s*. Salt Lake City: Salt Lake Art Center, 1965.

History of Idaho Territory, Showing Its Resources and Advantages; With Illustrations Descriptive of Its Scenery... San Francisco, Wallace W. Elliott & Company, 1884. Reprinted Fairfield, Washington: Ye Galleon Press, 1973.

Huntley, James L. *Ferry Boats in Idaho*. Caldwell, Idaho: Caxton Printers, 1979.

The Idaho Encyclopedia. Compiled by the Federal Writers' Project of the Works Progress Administration; Vardis Fisher, State Director. Caldwell, Idaho: Caxton Printers, 1938.

Idaho; An Illustrated History. Boise: Idaho State Historical Society, 1976.

Island in the Snake: The Idaho Paintings of Pioneer Artist J. P. McMeekin. Boise: Idaho Historical Museum, 1983.

Kovinick, Phil. *The Woman Artist in the American West, 1860-1960*. Fullerton, California: Muckenthaler Cultural Center, 1976.

McCracken, Harold. *Great Painters and Illustrators of the Old West*. New York: Dover, 1988.

Magnusson, Brian B. *Under Western Skies: A Tribute to the Art of Olaf Moller*. Seattle: Nordic Heritage Museum, 1987.

Maguire, James H. *Mary Hallock Foote*. Western Writers Series, no. 2. Boise: Boise State College, 1972.

Marling, Karal Ann. *Wall-To-Wall America; A Cultural History of Post-Office Murals in the Great Depression*. Minneapolis: University of Minnesota Press, 1982.

Montgomery, Feodora L. *My Father, Feodor Von Luerzer*. Coeur d'Alene, Idaho: n.p., 1973.

Nicandri, David L. *Northwest Chiefs; Gustav Sohon's Views of the 1855 Stevens Treaty Councils*. Tacoma: Washington State Historical Society, 1986.

Nolan, Edward W. *Frank Palmer, Scenic Photographer*. Spokane: Eastern Washington State Historical Society, 1987.

Nolan, Edward W. *A Guide to the Cutter Collection*. Spokane: Eastern Washington State Historical Society, 1984.

Nolan, Edward W. *Northern Pacific Views; The Railroad Photography of F. Jay Haynes*, 1876-1905. Helena: Montana Historical Society Press, 1983.

Northwest History in Art, 1778-1963. Pacific Northwest Historical Pamphlet, no. 3. Tacoma: Washington State Historical Society, 1963.

Park, Marlene. *Democratic Vistas: Post Offices and Public Art in the New Deal*. Philadelphia: Temple University Press, 1984.

Paul, Rodman W. *When Culture Came to Boise: Mary Hallock Foote in Idaho*. Idaho Historical Series, no. 19. Boise: Idaho State Historical Society, 1977.

Pioneer Idaho Artist Charles L. Ostner. Idaho Historical Series, no. 15. Boise: Idaho State Historical Society, 1966.

Point, Nicolas. *Wilderness Kingdom; Indian Life in the Rocky Mountains: 1840-1847; the Journals and Paintings of Nicolas Point, S.J.* Trans. and intro. by Joseph P. Donnelly. New York: Holt, Rinehart & Winston, 1967.

Preuss, Charles. *Exploring with Fremont; The Private Diaries of Charles Preuss, Cartographer*. Trans. and ed. by Erwin G. and Elisabeth K. Gudde. Norman: University of Oklahoma Press, 1958.

Public Works of Art Project. *Report of the Assistant Secretary of the Treasury to Federal Emergency Relief Administrator, December 8, 1933 - June 30, 1934*. Washington, D.C.: U.S. Government Printing Office, 1934.

Reps, John W. *Panoramas of Promise; Pacific Northwest Cities and Towns on Nineteenth-Century Lithographs*. Pullman: Washington State University Press, 1984.

Reps, John W. *Views and Viewmakers of Urban America; Lithographs of Towns and Cities in the United States and Canada, Notes of the Artists and Publishers, and a Union Catalog of their Work, 1825-1925*. Columbia: University of Missouri Press, 1984.

Rossi, Paul A. *The Art of the Old West, from the Collection of the Gilcrease Institute*. New York: Knopf, 1971.

Samuels, Peggy and Harold. *Illustrated Biographical Encyclopedia of Artists of the American West*. Garden City, New York: Doubleday, 1976.

Schwantes, Carlos A. *The Pacific Northwest; An Interpretive History*. Lincoln: University of Nebraska Press, 1989.

Shipman, Nell. *The Silent Screen & My Talking Heart; An Autobiography*. Hemingway Western Studies Series. Boise: Boise State University, 1987.

Stenzel, Franz. *James Madison Alden: Yankee Artist of the Pacific Coast*. Fort Worth, Texas: Amon Carter Museum, 1975.

Stevens, Isaac I. *Narrative and Final Report of Explorations for a Route for a Pacific Railroad near the Forty-seventh and Forty-ninth Parallels of North Latitude, from St. Paul to Puget Sound*. Illustrations by J. M. Stanley and G. Sohon. Reports of Explorations and Surveys...Mississippi River to the Pacific Ocean, 1853-5; Volume 12, book 1. Washington, D.C.: Thomas H. Ford, Printer, 1860.

Trenton, Patricia, and Peter H. Hassrick. *The Rocky Mountains; A Vision for Artists in the Nineteenth Century*. Published in association with the Buffalo Bill Historical Center, Cody, Wyoming. Norman: University of Oklahoma, 1983.

Tyler, Ron. *Alfred Jacob Miller: Artist on the Oregon Trail*. With a Catalogue Raisonne by Karen Dewees Reynolds and William R. Johnston. Fort Worth, Texas: Amon Carter Museum, 1982.

Wheeler, Keith. *The Chroniclers*. The Old West Series. Alexandria, Virginia: Time-Life Books, 1976.

Wilkins, James F. *An Artist on the Overland Trail: The 1849 Diary and Sketches of James F. Wilkins*. San Marino, California: Huntington Library, 1968.

Wright, Patricia and Lisa B. Reitzes. *Tourtellotte and Hummel of Idaho: The Standard Practice of Architecture*. Logan: Utah State University Press, 1987.

PERIODICALS

Hart, Arthur. "Painter of Idaho Indians" [Helen Hoff Aupperle]. *Incredible Idaho* 3(Fall 1971):10-14.

Hawley, Jody. "Nick Villeneuve, Idaho's Cartoonist." *Idaho Yesterdays* 31(Winter 1988):24-32.

Hibbard, Don. "Chicago 1893: Idaho at the World's Columbian Exposition." *Idaho Yesterdays* 24(Summer 1980): 24-29.

Hults, Linda C. "Thomas Moran's Shoshone Falls; A Western Niagara." *Smithsonian Studies in American Art* 3(Winter 1989):89-102.

Nottage, James H. "A Centennial History of Artist Activities in Wyoming, 1837-1937." *Annals of Wyoming* 48(Spring 1976):77-100.

Ostrogorsky, Michael. "Fort Boise and the 'New Confederacy': Vigilantes, Indians, and Copperheads." *Idaho Yesterdays* 23(Spring 1979):18-31.

Potera, Carol. "Down-to-Earth" [Don Bemco Bennett]. *Valley Magazine* (Summer 1986):25-27.

Rasmussen, Louise. "Artists of the Explorations Overland, 1840-1860." *Oregon Historical Quarterly* 43(March 1942): 56-62.

Whiting, Henry. "Teater's Knoll: The Wright Stuff." *Idaho Arts Journal* (March/April 1988):12.

Wilkinson, Augusta. "Art in Idaho." *American Magazine of Art* 18(May 1927):270-71.

NEWSPAPER ARTICLES

Ainscough, M. W. "Northwest History Told in Art" [Rowena Alcorn]. *News Tribune* [Tacoma] June 26, 1974.

"Artists' Exhibit Opens Next Week at Heyburn, Idaho." *Idaho Daily Statesman* March 4, 1934.

Hall, Utahna L. "Idaho City Charms Artists Since Days of Gold Rush." *Statewide* [Boise] December 27, 1951:6.

________. "Idaho City Artist: Maggie Brown." *Idaho World* [Idaho City] July 2, 1980:1.

Hart, Arthur. "Early Artist Drew Mining Camps" [E. Greene]. *Idaho Statesman* June 12, 1978:4A.

________. "Early Artists Earned Praise, But Little Cash." *Idaho Statesman* April 19, 1984:5D.

________. "1884 Book of History Enhanced by Artists." *Idaho Statesman* July 22, 1974:15.

________. "Frontier Artists Had to Rough It." *Idaho Statesman* May 29, 1978:6B.

________. "Frontier Life Didn't Keep Artists From Seeking the Spirit of Idaho." *Idaho Statesman* June 5, 1978:4A.

________. "Grove Street Mansion Housed 1892 Art Exhibit." *Idaho Statesman* August 14, 1989:3D.

________. "'Hogan the Stiff' Makes Mark in Boise Annals." *Idaho Statesman* September 7, 1970:8.

________. "Pioneer Artists Preserved Grandeur of Territorial Idaho." *Idaho Statesman* December 13, 1976:11A.

________. "Today's Museum Pieces Were Yesterday's Fair Entries." *Idaho Statesman* August 7, 1989:3D.

"Idaho Works of Art for Public Display." *Capital News* [Boise] April 24, 1934.

Jones, Bonnie Baird. "Teater Paints World From Home." *Idaho Statesman* July 8, 1976, "The 43rd Star" supplement:43.

Kissane, Leedice. "Story of West: Artist's Destiny" [Minerva Teichert]. *Idaho State Journal* [Pocatello] October 31, 1982:2C.

"National Gallery of Art Honors Idaho Falls Artist with Award" [Helen Aupperle]. *Post-Register* [Idaho Falls] March 11, 1966:3.

"Portrait of a Distinguished Citizen" [Cornelia Hart Farrer]. *Idaho Statesman* September 3, 1972:5A.

Powers, Peggy. "The Creative Spirit of Art is Mathews." *Daily Universe* [Provo,Utah] December 2, 1968:6.

"Reminiscing With Old Folks: Douglas Knox of Emmett." *Idaho Daily Statesman* July 24, 1932.

Taylor, Suzanne. "First Idaho State Seal: A Woman's Handiwork; the Story of Emma Edwards Green." *Idaho Statesman* July 2, 1972:2C.

Varian, Nina. "Artist Plans Boise Murals" [Fletcher Martin]. *Idaho Daily Statesman* February 5, 1939.

Warbis, Mark. "Historical Museum to Show Off Idahoan's Editorial Cartoons." *Idaho Statesman* December 22, 1986:3C.

Warnick, David. "Take For Instance, the Value of Art Compared with Dirty Towels" [Arnold Westerlund]. *Lewiston Morning Tribune* July 11, 1976:4C.

Whitacre, Dianne. "River Town Mourns Loss of Old House" [Harry Parnell]. *Idaho Statesman* November 21, 1977:1B.

Williams, Walter M. "The Story of the Pioneer Idaho Woman Who Designed the Great Seal of the State" [Emma Edwards Green]. *Idaho Daily Statesman* January 30, 1949:8B.

INDEX

Addison, Robert William 103, 117
Alcorn, Rowena 82, 117
Alden, James Madison 22, 117
Aupperle, Helen Hoff 91, 117
Barnard, Thomas Nathan 53, 117
Bennett, Don Bemco 108, 117
Berryman, Clifford K. 118
Black, Mary Elizabeth 37, 118
Bowman, Sara Annette 77, 118
Bradley, Mrs. M. J. 48, 118
Brown, Benjamin Chambers 85, 118
Brown, Margaretta Favorite 26, 118
Burbank, Elbridge Ayer 44, 118
Burris, Fanny Dike 93, 118
Carey, W. M. 118
Cartee, La Fayette 118
Castle, James 94, 118
Catlin, George 18, 118
Chester, Idella Rogers 72, 119
Chester, Ruperta 73, 119
Coleman, C. Emma 9, 119
Collins, Herbert A. 63, 119
Crombe, E. 54, 119
Culmer, Henry L. A. 47, 119
Cutter, Kirtland Kelsey 66, 119
Denton, Wilma 119
Dunn, Alfred 111, 119
Elliott, Wallace W. 39, 119
Euler, Reeves 100, 120
Farrer, Cornelia Hart 99, 120
Fery, John 56, 120
Finnigan, Minnie 120
Flammia, Patrick 114, 120
Foote, Mary Hallock 58, 120
Fowler, Ethel Lucile 96, 120
Frank Leslie's Illustrated Newspaper 34, 120
Gibbs, George 16, 120
Gilbert 75, 120
Gray, U. L. 40, 120
Green, Emma Edwards 62, 120
Greene, Edmond 32, 121
Harper's Weekly 35, 121
Haynes, Frank Jay 49, 121
Hill, Abby Williams 57, 121
Hincelin, Arm 23, 121
Houghton, Merritt Dana 55, 121
Irvin, Marie 76, 121
Itter, Julian E. 60, 122
Jackson, William Henry 33, 122
Johnson, Frank Tenney 43, 122
Kirkwood, Mary 104, 122
Klinge, Nellie Kilgore 98, 122
Koch, Augustus 50, 122
Lauder, Minnie Taylor 122
Limbert, Robert W 74, 122
Lyon, Caleb 122
McIntosh, Mr. & Mrs. Walter 45, 122
McMeekin, Joseph Patrick 68, 122
Martin, Fletcher 101, 123
Mathews, Conan 115, 123
Miller, Alfred Jacob 6, 11, 123
Moller, Oscar Olaf 92, 123
Moore, Agnes Randall 97, 123
Moran, Peter 28, 123
Moran, Thomas 25, 29, 123
Neilson, Thomas Raymond 109, 123
Ostner, Charles 30, 124
Palmer, Frank 70, 124
Parnell, Harry 102, 124
Parrish, Ella Knox 38, 124
Parrott, William Samuel 124
Parson, Oliver 110, 124
Point, Nicolas 12, 124
Postle, Katherine Joy 84, 125
Preuss, Charles 15, 125
Rayburn, H. S. 125
Remington, Frederic 42, 125
Richter, Agnes Bowen 36, 125
Roberts, George 113, 125
Schroeder, George Eugene 81, 125
Shipley, George E. 125
Shipman, Nell 80, 125
Slight, T. 51, 125
Smith, Cecil Alden 88, 125
Smith, Edward 41, 125
Smith, W. Thomas 67, 126
Sohon, Gustavus 20, 126
Spalding, Eliza 82, 126
Spielman, Samuel 126
Stanley, John Mix 19, 126
Stockbridge, Nellie 52, 117
Stoops, Herbert Morton 87, 126
Stuart, Granville 126
Stuart, James Everett 46, 126
Tappan, William 17, 126
Teater, Archie Boyd 106, 126
Teichert, Minerva 90, 126
Tourtellotte & Hummel, Architects 64, 127
Villeneuve, Nick 86, 127
Von Luerzer, Feodor 71, 127
Walton, Richard Guy 78
Westerlund, Arnold 112, 127
West Shore Magazine 127
Wilkins, James F. 14, 127

ACKNOWLEDGMENTS

The exhibition and catalog of *One Hundred Years of Idaho Art: 1850-1950* were made possible by the combined efforts and assistance of many individuals. We are particularly indebted to the artists, galleries, museums, and private collectors who have graciously lent their support and artwork to this exhibition.

We are extremely grateful to the staff of the Idaho State Historical Society, whose cooperation enabled this project to become a reality. We extend our gratitude especially to Jody Hawley, Joe Toluse, and Ken Swanson, who provided invaluable assistance with the loan of numerous works. We wish to thank Judy Austin for her editorial suggestions and guidance regarding the historical accuracy of the catalog; and Elizabeth Jacox, Guila Ford, Larry Jones, and John Yandell for their thoughtful advice.

Throughout the organization of this exhibition, we have received the encouragement and support of many colleagues and friends who have been generous with their time and knowledge. Among those who deserve special recognition are: Susan Buchel, Nez Perce Historical Park; Joanne Jones, Latah County Historical Society; Mr. and Mrs. John Fery; Barbara Frentress, Boise Basin Museum; John Guido and Tina Oswald, Washington State University Library; Marilyn Hansen; Johanna Hays, Prichard Gallery, University of Idaho; Charles Hummel of Hummel, LaMarche & Hunsucker, Architects; Tambra Johnson, Library of Congress; Nan Farrington Jones; Mary Kirkwood; Jim Kolva, Eastern Washington University; Gregg Losinski, Idaho State University; Glenn Mason, Beth Sellars, Larry Schoonover, Ed Nolan, and Lynn Harrison of Eastern Washington State Historical Society and Cheney Cowles Museum; Lynn Melton, Boise Public Library; Kerry Moosman; Larry Peters, Sidestreet Gallery; George Roberts; Jack Spurgeon; Tom Trusky, Boise State University; Lynn Webster, Rosenthal Gallery of Art; Arnold Westerlund; Janice Wigen, Museum of Native American Cultures; and Wally Yates, Yates-Fritchman Galleries.

One Hundred Years of Idaho Art could not be achieved without the collaboration of the Boise Art Museum staff, who generously provided their time toward the success of this project. We offer our sincere appreciation to Dennis O'Leary, executive director, for his enthusiastic support; Barbara Streng, administrator, for her patience and efforts toward catalog production and grant administration; and Alberta Mayo, assistant director, for her help with editing. Our thanks also go to Richard Young, curator of education; Nancy McDaniel, community development coordinator; Ron Walker, preparator; and Merita Nate, receptionist, for their contributions to the project. A very special thank you is offered to Jen Ray, registrar, for coordinating loan insurance, transportation, framing, and photography arrangements. We acknowledge the work of two dedicated volunteers: Peggy Gledhill for manuscript editing, and Alma Frith for aid with catalog preparation. We are also indebted to David Airhart for his sensitive framing of works, Michael Cordell for photography, and Geoff Beard for his handsome catalog design.

We are grateful to the generous sponsors of the exhibition whose commitment made this endeavor possible: Albertson's, Inc., Beaux Arts Société, Idaho Centennial Commission, Idaho Humanities Council, Key Bank of Idaho, and the National Endowment for the Arts. In addition we would like to warmly thank the Board of Trustees for their confidence and support of this project.

Lastly, we express our gratitude to Ed Cryer and Gary Bettis for their patience and understanding throughout the past year.

Sandy Harthorn
Kathleen Bettis

BOARD OF TRUSTEES 1990 - 1991

STAFF 1990-1991

DENNIS O'LEARY, EXECUTIVE DIRECTOR

ALBERTA MAYO, ASSISTANT DIRECTOR

SANDY HARTHORN, CURATOR OF EXHIBITIONS

RICHARD A. YOUNG, CURATOR OF EDUCATION

BARBARA J. STRENG, ADMINISTRATOR

NANCY MCDANIEL, COMMUNITY DEVELOPMENT COORDINATOR

JEN KAY, REGISTRAR

KATHY BETTIS, CURATORIAL ASSISTANT

RONALD WALKER, PREPARATOR

MERITA NATE, RECEPTIONIST

DEBORAH A. MASON, ACCOUNTING ASSISTANT

VIRGIL STEWART, CUSTODIAN

ALMA FRITH, CURATORIAL VOLUNTEER

ELINOR THOMAS, ADMINISTRATIVE VOLUNTEER

DOROTHY MILLARD, VOLUNTEER LIBRARIAN

MUSEUM STORE

TAMARA FRICKE

CHERRILL HYATT

LAURA RAGAN

CATHERINE RAKOW

PHOTOGRAPH CREDITS

PHOTOGRAPHS NOT ACKNOWLEDGED IN THE FOLLOWING LIST HAVE BEEN SUPPLIED BY THE OWNERS OR CUSTODIANS OF THE WORKS:

HILLEL BURGER: PAGE 16

MICHAEL CORDELL: PAGES 9, 22, 23, 24, 26, 27, 30, 31, 32, 36, 37, 38, 40, 41, 43, 45, 51, 54, 55, 63, 64, 65, 66, 67, 69, 71, 81, 82, 83, 84, 86, 88, 89, 90, 91, 93, 98, 100, 102, 103, 104, 105, 107, 108, 109, 110, 111, 113

THE DARK ROOM: PAGES 15, 17, 20, 34, 35, 39, 72, 74, 75, 76, 77, 94, 95, 97, 112

MEDIA SPECIALTIES: PAGES 99, 111